W9-APM-866

"A leader leads by example,
whether he or she intends to or not."
– *Anonymous*

"**David Grossman has developed proven, thoughtful communication methodologies that help leaders succeed in their everyday and defining moments. Like a football coach calling a play based on game conditions, David's** leader**communicator™ Platform tool ensures leaders use the right message at the right time with the right audience, clearly and consistently. And in *You Can't Not Communicate*, David lays out the "Xs" and "Os" for building the communication skills necessary to win in today's business environment.**"

— *Steve Gillman, Executive Director of Health, Safety and Environment, Lilly*

"David's smart, sincere and thoughtful approach models the strategies he advocates. To sit and speak with David is to get a healthy dose of communication 101, whether one is a novice or an aspiring expert. **As I transitioned from a senior management role to executive director, David's wisdom guided me, and continues to shape my approach to many aspects of my work.**"

— *Dr. Jeff Boehm, Executive Director, The Marine Mammal Center*

"The corporate world has experienced so much change in recent years—from economic upheaval to heightened societal expectations to the emergence of new technologies and new media—that you'd think leaders would have learned how to manage it.

But the reality is that many of those in leadership positions—from supervisors to CEOs—continue to underestimate the quantity and quality of communication necessary to guide their organizations through an ever-changing business landscape. Fortunately, David Grossman has produced a book that reminds leaders of the importance of getting communication right, and more important, provides them with the tools they need to master the communications challenge."

— *Paul Holmes, Editor and Publisher, The Holmes Report*

"In my role as a corporate psychologist focused on the effectiveness of organizations, teams, and leaders, I have had the chance to work closely with David and see his expertise and insights make significant differences both for leaders and for his own team.

David 'practices what he preaches' and shows that his pragmatic approach can be used by leaders of all levels. Whether a leader has limited time or limited communications training, *You Can't Not Communicate* shares some of David's best thinking for leveraging communications strategically and realistically to enhance results and to ensure overall engagement."

— *Dr. Ginger Hale, President, Hale Consulting, LLC*

"Effective communication is essential in every organization today. David's words not only engage and inspire leaders at a visionary level, but he also provides a host of pragmatic strategies that are easy to implement and applicable to organizations of all sizes and types. **Leaders committed to their own development as well as the success of their organizations 'can't not' read this important book.**"

— *Dr. Thomas Hagerman, Superintendent, River Forest School District*

"Trust is central to effective leadership communication and there is no more trustworthy advisor on the topic than David Grossman. **He offers practical advice that is immediately actionable—advice that may sound so simple that you wonder why you didn't think of it yourself. That's the magic of** *You Can't Not Communicate*. **Leaders who read this book will find themselves experiencing many "aha" moments.**"

— *Sally Benjamin Young, Vice President, Communications, Lundbeck Inc.*

"At McDonald's, relationships matter as much as results. David's approach to leadership communication underscores the importance of both because it helps business leaders do the right things *right*. I've seen first-hand the power of David's methods in action through his long-standing work with McDonald's. David and his team have been instrumental in elevating leaders' influence to drive further action and results.

This book is a window into David's world of proven and practical insights, methods and tools that have made him a highly effective leader, business owner, and coach to other business leaders. I'd encourage every professional looking to get to the next level to read David's book."

— *Richard P. Ellis, Senior Vice President, Communications & Public Affairs, McDonald's Restaurants of Canada Limited / President & CEO, Ronald McDonald House Charities of Canada*

"David Grossman takes the common sense of great communication and provides the tools, techniques, and motivation to help every business leader—from supervisor to CEO—make it common practice."

— *Patricia M. Crull, Ph.D., Vice President, Chief Learning Officer, Time Warner Cable*

2ND Edition

YOU CAN'T **NOT** COMMUNIC**A**TE

*Proven Communication Solutions
that Power the Fortune 100*

HOW TOP LEADERS **DIFFERENTIATE THEMSELVES**

by DAVID GROSSMAN, ABC, APR, Fellow PRSA

Copyright © 2012, 2009 Little Brown Dog Publishing

No part of this book may be reproduced, stored in a retrieval system, or transmitted by any means without the written permission of the author.

ISBN: 978-0-615-62297-2

Library of Congress Control Number: 2012937607

Printed in the United States of America.
This book is printed on acid-free paper.

Images provided by iStockphoto.com, all rights reserved.

To Steve, who always saves me the best seat in the house.
Right next to him.

The Power and Purpose of Effective Communication

Traveling to many of the 33,000 McDonald's restaurants in 118 countries around the world, I see every day the impact good communication can have on our organization, and what happens under the Golden Arches when communication doesn't go well. How well we communicate can make the difference in our ability to deliver a true McDonald's experience—we call it an *I'm lovin' it*® experience—to every customer, every time, anywhere in the world.

Communication Must be Purposeful and Inclusive

I first realized the importance of communication early in my McDonald's career when I was assigned to lead field operations in the Detroit region. Having started as a crew member in 1973, I had risen through the ranks and managed mostly by directing people to get the job done. When it came time to lead a sizable team, I had a rude awakening. My very direct style didn't work very well for some folks.

I thought communication meant telling people what to do. Over time, I realized that the only way to get things done is through people. And the best way to do that is by motivating, engaging, and inspiring individuals. No one likes being told what to do, including me. Effective communication requires influence, and being

Over the past 30 years, I've seen McDonald's evolve from an entirely "get it done" culture to one dependent on influence and inclusion. How we work together matters—getting the right things done right, in the right way, at the right time. Especially on the tough issues—in areas where our company and people focus significant resources and attention—we need to ensure there's input and engagement up front—whether it's from our owner/operator leadership, various global boards and councils, or our supplier partners, among others.

Process Helps Realize the Potential

In working with David Grossman—both as a colleague at McDonald's and after he created The Grossman Group—I've come to realize that everything you do or say, every action you take, sends a message. It's up to you to choose to be purposeful in the messages you send, or to wing it and reduce your chances of success.

With help from David and my global communications team, I now know the potential—and the important work involved—in purposeful communication. As Worldwide Chief Restaurant Officer, I'm always thinking about the landscape of our industry and what McDonald's must do to continue its strong growth and further deliver on our strategy, which is called the *Plan to Win*. Our opportunity is to ignite the power of the McDonald's system to make it REAL in the restaurants. We never lose sight of the fact that at the end of the day, all our work is about delivering at the moment of truth, which is the transaction at the front counter and in the drive-thru. It's all about the customer.

As we thought about how my team could do an even better job of supporting the system, we went through the process of identifying the need for change, discussing how we could influence the change that was required, and identifying the results we were looking for. We determined the gaps that needed to be filled and became selective on the strategies and actions to deploy. Once we had the plan in place, we focused on how we could best tell the story of what's possible and what I personally needed to do to lead the effort. This became my messaging platform, and the centerpiece of all my communications.

In following this approach over the years, I learned that purposeful communication requires more time and thought than the average type-A leader might typically think. Even with a thoughtful plan and platform, it is easy to fall back into old habits like being too direct and not listening. Today I'm more aware of when I need to take a step back, take a deep breath, and evaluate a response before I take action to be sure it will truly meet the system's goals and my intentions.

Over the past decade, this approach has helped us align the Restaurant Solutions Group as a global team that consistently meets its goals with an eye on continuous improvement. After years of focused communication, and a lot of hard work, we are aligned better today then ever before as a global team.

Communication Builds Community

When I think about communication at its finest, I picture a very special priest at Old St. Patrick's Church in Chicago who I've watched for the last few years. In the moments before his sermon, he seems so focused on his message he doesn't hear what's going on around him. Then, when he gets up to speak, he always seems to be talking directly to every person in the church.

I asked him once who he envisions talking to when he speaks to the congregation. I'll never forget his answer: "I'm not talking to those in the so-called 'in crowd' that I see every Sunday. I'm talking to the people I don't know because that's the only way I can connect with them to make them feel welcome."

Father John Cusick is creating a community by connecting with people— especially those he doesn't know. I believe this is a valuable lesson for those of us leading organizations.

As leaders, we need to create a sense of community where employees feel welcome and connected, and know they're part of something special where they can make a true difference. It means we need to connect in a real way with people.

When we think about what we'll say and how we'll say it, we need to consider how it will impact the last hired employee, the ones we don't know yet, and those we will influence in the future. We need to be willing to accept that everything we do, everything we say, everything we don't do and everything we don't say speaks volumes.

I've truly learned that you can't not communicate. The work behind purposeful communication is well worth it when you see the kind of impact we can have on individuals, our teams, and our business.

Jeff Stratton
Executive Vice President and Worldwide Chief Restaurant Officer

One thing hasn't changed since I first wrote *"You Can't **NOT** Communicate"*—effective communication remains the secret to business success. I've never been more convinced. Yet for most leaders, this is a significant blind spot that derails relationships, make goals harder to achieve, limits advancement opportunities, and impedes overall business and personal success.

Leaders might think they are communicating effectively, but research with employees tells a different story. Employees don't trust the very leaders who are running global organizations today. They're skeptical and confused about their role and how they fit in. While they value their supervisors, many employees don't have the information they need to do their jobs well. Consequently, they're neutral or, worse yet, disengaged.

Here's what many leaders don't realize: they are already communicating whether they intend to or not. It's human nature for others to read into our actions based on their perceptions. And as we know, actions speak louder than words.

So if we're communicating with or without intention, which is the premise of this book, my thought for every leader is to get good at it.

*"You Can't **NOT** Communicate"* is full of proven strategies that work, which can be implemented today. This second edition contains two chapters that are new. For those leaders who are still not convinced of the value of communication, chapter 1 contains the latest data on the bottom-line benefits of communication, and the paralyzing costs of ineffective communication.

Second, I'm continually reminded of the difficulty leaders have in developing and articulating strategy, which employees need to bring to life. Chapter 11 reviews the common mistakes that many CEOs and senior leaders make as they work to turn strategy into a reality for their employees, and what they can do about it.

One final caveat—as you read through this book, keep the following in mind: knowing how to do something doesn't mean you can do it. If you think the strategies and tips included are "helpful reminders," ask yourself how you demonstrate the skill mentioned, and whether you can apply it in various situations, in different settings, and with diverse audiences. That's one of the true signs of mastery. In addition, once you've become more effective at communication, there are always ways to raise the bar.

May your improved communications bring you even greater success.

David Grossman, ABC, APR, Fellow PRSA

Founder & CEO

The Grossman Group

{ ACKNOWLEDGEMENTS }

I'm grateful to many people who have inspired me, challenged me, taught me, and opened my eyes to all that's possible when communication is done well. For the leaders who leverage this superpower called communication every day, I know the hard work it takes to communicate effectively. Thank you for being a role model to others, and for giving employees what they want and deserve—the information and inspiration they need to contribute and feel great about their ability to make a difference.

To my mentors and teachers, thank you for being open to my countless and sometimes relentless questions as I sought answers to so many "whys?" Please know that my toddler is just as curious, and asks almost as many questions as I did.

To our clients who entrust their business challenges in us and who partner with us so we can do great work. I'm grateful for the opportunity and never forget the trust you put in us.

To the **thought**partners™ at The Grossman Group, you are truly the "get-it-done" team, and your commitment to our values sets us apart from the pack.

To my family, I'm grateful for the support to continue to do what I love.

And for my darling daughter, Avi, being your Dad is a wonderful gift. The wait for you has been worth it, and I'm only starting to know how much.

"I don't have time to communicate."
That's one of the most common myths
I hear from business leaders.

The reality is that everything leaders do
communicates—whether they want it to
or not; how they spend their time, what
they focus on, who they interact with, the
employees they recognize, and so on.

The reality is that
you can't ***not*** communicate.

So, if you're communicating whether you want to or not, why not ensure your communications are driving the business results you want?

What if I told you there are simple but effective communication strategies that will increase your visibility and impact, along with your business results? These same strategies are proven to help you get promoted and move up the ladder.

We've entered the dawn of the leader**communicator**™. Even though there hasn't been a news flash on CNN or the national networks, leaders are realizing—through research, listening to thought leaders, and listening to employees—they have a role that may be more important than presiding at board meetings, minding budgets, or ensuring succession planning.

Their most important role in the organization is making sure that employees "get it," that they understand how to connect the dots between the overarching business strategy and goals of the organization, and the ways in which each individual's day-to-day work contributes to achieving success. A leader's ability to engage and connect each and every employee to the organization is key to achieving performance and long-term goals.

Just because you're a business leader, however, doesn't mean you know how to communicate. In fact, communication is a learned skill. Having worked with leaders at all levels in various Fortune 100 companies and industries across the globe, it's a truism that very few of them were promoted because of their communication skills. They were strong individual contributors who achieved business results, and they now need to engage and influence others; new and challenging skills.

Today, you can't separate communications from leadership much like you can't separate leadership from results. Communication is the way we do business. This book is designed to help leaders solve three of the toughest challenges they face:

- Minimize the downside of change where business could be interrupted, slowed, or stopped

- Turn employee apathy, confusion, and skepticism into greater engagement and productivity

- Maximize the upside of change and accelerate the achievement of business results

The strategies in these pages have been built on the Grossman Methodology, which encompasses The Grossman Group's proprietary tools, training and **thought**partner approach, and have been proven by countless leaders and clients of ours from the Fortune 100. These time-tested solutions will help you inspire, motivate and engage your employees and get the business results you want and deserve. More and more, that makes internal communication one of the most valuable investments today's business leaders can make.

Remember: no one is more influential than the leader, and that gives you both the responsibility and the opportunity to inspire your workforce to reach new heights in business results. And, those of you who do will rise to the top, because you know you can't *not* communicate.

Who is this ideal leader**communicator**
and what does he or she know?

From research with dozens of our
Fortune 100 clients around the globe,
we pulled together the core components
every leader should exemplify.

leader**communicator** *(lédr • komûni-kàtor)* ***n.***

1. understands communication begins and ends with himself or herself **2.** understands that communication is an instrument of strategy, and a strategy in itself **3.** meets employees' strategic communication needs **4.** plans communication; is aware communication doesn't just "happen" **5.** ensures actions follow words; knows people search for meaning in actions **6.** recognizes that most problems in business today lie in the absence of real communication, and facilitates dialogue to create shared meaning

© The Grossman Group

{ leader**communicator** }

The Business of Communicating

Starting thought

Communication tools: Luxury good or bare necessity?

I was reviewing some of The Grossman Group's tools with a leader who thought a messaging methodology or leadership platform was a "luxury," like "GPS or electric seat warmers." (Though, believe me, to survive the harsh Chicago winters, seat warmers are not a luxury; they're a necessity!)

A strategic approach to communications, too, is a necessity. The fact that he mentioned GPS was ironic to me. Nothing is more important today to employees than an understanding of where their organization is going and the plans to get there. Without understanding that, employees can't connect the dots to figure out how they fit in (and why they should contribute the extra brainpower, time, and energy that every organization needs today).

I'm sure you follow a specific process when you develop strategic plans in your organization, report financials, or manage succession planning. Why should communications be different? Is it any less important or valuable?

One thing I know for sure is that senior leaders struggle with developing and articulating strategy at the highest level. Even the best leaders are challenged with translating the plans that were painstakingly created in the boardroom to make them relevant to the individuals who will bring them to life. Or not.

I've had the "luxury" to see the great power and results of world-class communications.

When you don't know where you're going, you'll never get there—with or without GPS.

Where are you headed today?

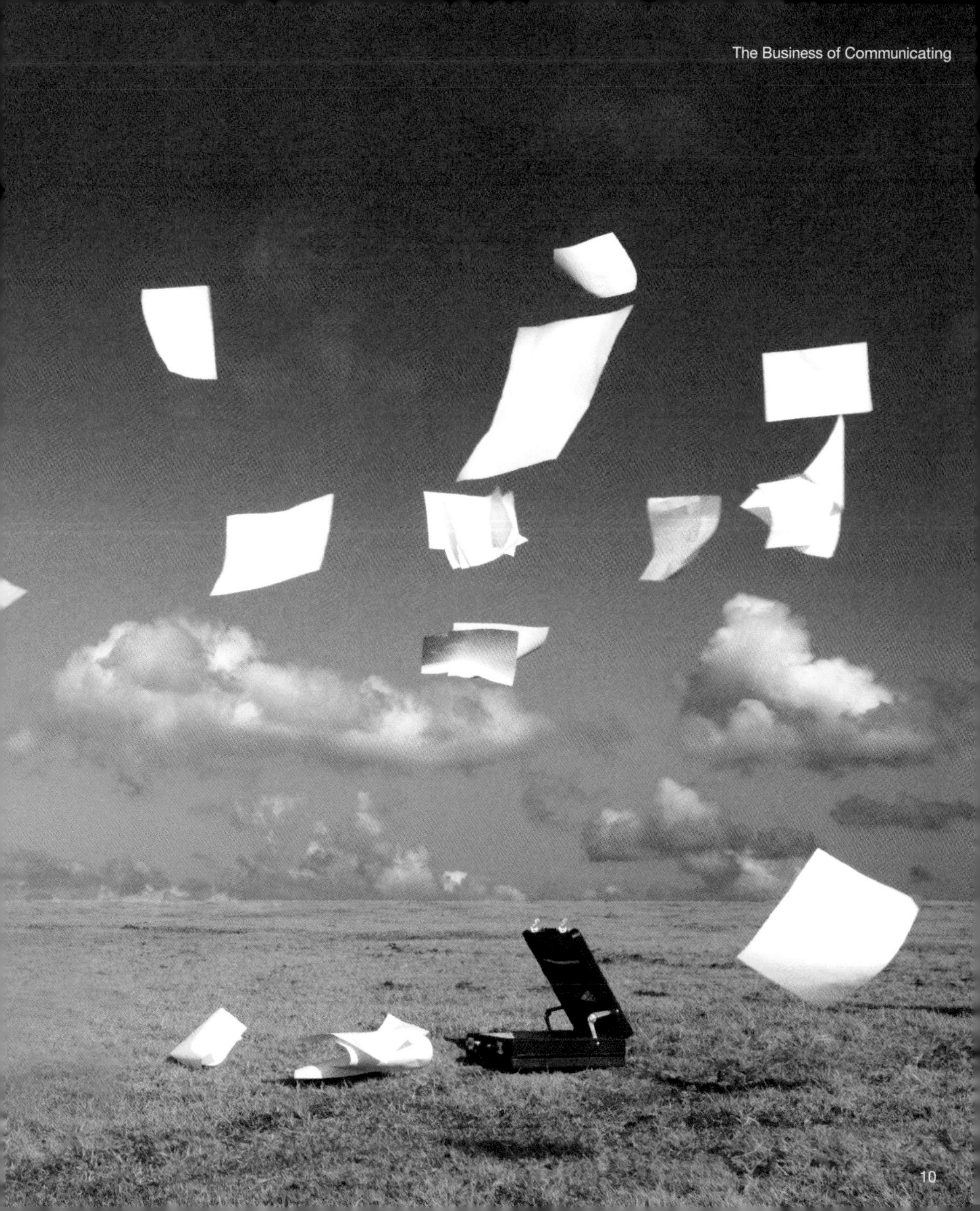

Communication Means Business

Communication is more than a "feel good" part of any organization. Great internal communication helps employees connect the dots between what they do and the overarching business strategy. When it's good, it informs. When it's great, it engages employees and moves them to action. Done right, communication helps people and organizations be even better.

Are One Third of Your Employees Planning to Leave?

Let's say that you knew that one third of current employees were planning on leaving you in the next five years. But that you could dramatically lower that number by engaging employees through communication. Would you be able to put a price on that? How much would that be worth to you? (I'll leave you to do the math...an average of $17,000/employee x Number of employees x 5 years...) Ouch! A lot, right?

But here's the reality:

Nearly one third of employees plan to move jobs within the next five years, according to the talent management company Lumesse, as detailed in their 2011 Global Workplace Survey.[1] Results showed that although overall engagement levels are good, more than 80 percent of employees feel their skills are not being fully utilized in the workplace, which could ultimately affect the high levels of expected turnover.

The survey, conducted among 4,000 employees, across 14 countries—including the US, UK, Germany and China—examined employee attitudes toward their jobs and employers in areas such as loyalty, job satisfaction, and workplace pride across all age groups. What the survey found just may surprise you (knowing that 29 percent of employees plan on changing jobs in the next five years):

- When asked, 69 percent of respondents reported being proud of where they work
- 60 percent said employer reputation was something that attracted them to their current job
- A shocking 81 percent of people said they don't feel their skills are being fully utilized in the workplace
- When asked about performance evaluations, 49 percent of respondents consider them to have little or no value

More specifically, the risk of talent loss is particularly high among employees ages 18-26 and 60 years and over:

- Almost half (46 percent) of 18- to 24-year-olds already have plans to leave their current job in the next five years. With this age group being such a large part of our workforce, this finding implies a lot of turnover, which could cost companies millions of dollars in time lost training new employees, lost productivity and lost intellectual capital.

- Fifty percent of employees ages 60 years and above, have reported a plan to switch jobs or leave the workforce within the next five years, which the survey points out, means losing the most experienced employees.

With such a high percentage of the workforce feeling that their skills aren't being used to their full potential, it comes as no surprise that people are looking to move to more challenging positions. Organizations will be especially vulnerable as economic conditions improve and employees have more choices.

The Bottom Line

Effective employee communication distinguishes great companies, propels outstanding leaders and generates excitement among employees.

Research confirms it also drives bottom-line results. Companies with highly effective communication practices had 47 percent higher total returns to shareholders over five years (2004-2009) compared to those with less effective communication.[2] It helps avoid the cost of misunderstanding, which refers to actions or errors of omission by employees who misunderstood, misinterpreted or were misinformed about company policies, business processes, job function or a combination of the three.

- An estimated $37 billion is lost annually in UK and US enterprises due to employee misunderstanding.[3]

- On average, employee misunderstanding costs a 100,000-employee company $62.4 million each year.[4]

- Misaligned communication costs small-and-medium-sized businesses (SMB) an average of $26,041 for every knowledge worker dealing with ineffective communication, and could cost a 100-employee company more than $500,000 a year.[5]

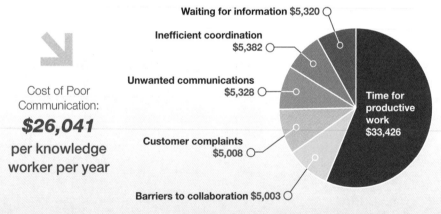

Cost of Poor Communication:

$26,041

per knowledge worker per year

Waiting for information $5,320

Inefficient coordination $5,382

Unwanted communications $5,328

Customer complaints $5,008

Barriers to collaboration $5,003

Time for productive work $33,426

Average compensation for a knowledge worker in an SMB is $59,467 per year

And it supports retention of talent.

- Employees who rate their companies' HR and talent programs as "world class" or "very good" are twice as committed to remaining at their jobs than employees who characterize those efforts as "fair" or "poor" (42 percent compared to 23 percent).[6]

Employee Engagement and Productivity

Multiple studies link employee engagement to retention, productivity, profitability and customer engagement—all drivers of business results. How leaders and the organization communicate is critical to engaging employees.

Engaged employees are more productive and present than their disengaged colleagues.

- Keeping employees engaged during times of change correlates to an average of 26 percent higher productivity rate.[7]

- Highly engaged employees miss fewer days of work and are three times as likely as their less-engaged peers to exceed performance expectations.[8]

- Employee engagement is linked to sales growth and customer engagement. In one research study, sales groups of highly engaged employees increased their overall percent of industry net sales by 24 percent, while less-engaged employee groups increased it by just 8 percent. The highly engaged group also had 8 percent higher customer engagement scores than the less-engaged group.[9]

Leader and manager communication is directly linked to employee engagement.

- Employee engagement rises when people experience a combination of effective and caring leadership, appealing development opportunities, interesting work, and fulfilling tangible and intangible rewards.[10]

- Employees are more engaged when they feel their immediate manager recognizes and appreciates good work. This factor alone was found to increase engagement by 60 percent in low-engagement workplaces and 20 percent in high-engagement workplaces.[11]

- Organizations that are highly effective communicators are three times more likely than the least effective communicators to train managers to deal openly with resistance to change.[12]

- A survey of 1,000 communications professionals found 44 percent said their supervisor strongly increased employee engagement and 50 percent reported disengagement due to poor employee morale and inadequate management and leadership.[13]

The Downside of Disengagement
There is a measurable downside to disengagement.

- In one study, nearly **half of 472 worldwide organizations (48 percent) reported their management had not effectively communicated business strategies to employees** in a way in which they could "live it in their daily jobs."[14]

- Not surprisingly, **only one-third (37 percent) of these organizations reported their employees were "effectively aligned to the missions and visions of their businesses."**[15]

- Nearly half of respondents (45 percent) in another survey of internal communicators said gaining leader and staff support is the scariest challenge they face.[16]

- 44 percent cited understanding leaders as the key variable to reducing fear and initiating positive action.[17]

- 45 percent said senior managers are a major block to progress in key areas of their development (far ahead of budgets and time pressures, at 19 percent each).[18]

What Happens When Employees Become Disengaged?[19]

More absenteeism—In a 10,000-person company, absenteeism due to disengagement results in about 5,000 lost days per year, which is valued at $600,000 in salary paid in which there was no work performed.

More turnover—Business units comprised of mostly disengaged employees have **31 percent** more turnover than those made up of mostly engaged employees.

More theft—Work groups with high numbers of disengaged employees lose **51 percent** more of their inventory

More injuries—Work groups with engagement scores on the bottom quartile average **62 percent** more accidents in the workplace.

Lower customer scores—Work groups with higher levels of engagement lead to **12 percent** higher customer scores than those on the lower end.

Lower productivity and profitability—Work groups in the top quartile of engagement are three times more likely to succeed, average **18 percent** higher productivity

Employee Trust and Influence

Trust and reputation go hand in hand, and research confirms that a company's relationship with its employees on the inside has everything to do with its reputation on the outside. Communication bridges the gaps.

Trust of corporations is eroding and adding to management challenges.

- An online poll of more than 1,800 adult employees in the U.S. found significant skepticism when it comes to trusting leaders and managers:[20]

    – Approximately one quarter (25 percent) of employees report having less trust in management than they did last year.

    – Only 10 percent of employees trust management to make the right decisions in times of uncertainty.

    – Just 14 percent of employees believe their company's leaders are ethical and honest.

    – Only 7 completely believe senior management's actions are completely consistent with their words.

- In another study, more than 40 percent of respondents were neutral or negative regarding their trust in supervisors.[21]

Organizations that treat employees well—and keep them informed—build stronger internal morale and external reputations.

- Research shows that treating employees well (63 percent) and communicating frequently (55 percent) are two of the five factors most important to corporate reputation after high quality products and services (69 percent), transparent and honest business practices (65 percent) and a company I can trust (65 percent).[22]

- When a company is trusted, 51 percent of people will believe positive information about it after one or two times hearing it, while 57 percent will believe negative information after hearing it one or two times when a company is distrusted.[23]

IBM: A Reputation Built on Trust
IBM commissioned a compelling study that demonstrates the value of the employee advocate to a company's external profile. [24]

The study, commissioned in seven countries,* asked respondents to share opinions of several major brands. One of the questions asked respondents to rank what has the biggest influence on their opinion of the companies they were asked about in the survey.

What were deemed most and least influential was consistent across the seven countries. Least influential were news stories, direct marketing and advertising. **Most influential—#1 in five of the seven countries and #2 in the other two—was "personal experiences with employees of that company."**

A subsequent study probed deeper on what was meant by "employee." Respondents did not just mean a company's sales person or customer-facing employee, but anyone who works—or worked—for that company. And for "personal experience," respondents didn't just mean face-to-face. They included online interactions, such as reading an individual's blog or being part of their social network.

*Brazil, Germany, Spain, Italy, India, Singapore, and Japan

"Honesty is the first chapter
in the book of wisdom."

– Thomas Jefferson

Three Reasons Why Engagement Matters

Reason #1:

Employees believe they can make a difference

A global study representing 85,000 employees of large and medium-sized companies revealed significant financial gains when organizations tap "employee performance potential."

The study found that more than three-quarters (84 percent) of highly engaged employees feel they can positively impact the quality of their company's products, whereas only 31 percent of the disengaged believe they have such an impact.

Only 19 percent of disengaged employees feel they can make a positive difference when it comes to costs in their work unit, whereas 68 percent of the highly engaged said they could positively impact costs.[25]

Reason #2:

The highly engaged create gains while the disengaged drain

The Center for Talent Solutions (CTS) estimates that when compared to normally engaged employees, the "fully engaged" employees deliver an average of 22 percent better performance, the "somewhat engaged" are typically about 75 percent as productive, and "disengaged employees" perform at about half the value.

Now, picture an organization of 25,000 employees in which 10 percent of the company is highly engaged, 64 percent are normally engaged, and 20 percent are highly disengaged. According to the CTS, this organization likely will lose about $112 million annually due to its less than engaged employees.[26] That's not pocket change.

Reason #3:

Companies drive better financial performance

Another study revealed a significant relationship between past employee engagement and present financial performance. For a company with a market value of $14 billion, an engaged workforce represents an increase in market value of 1.7 percent, which equates to $230 million.[27]

Dr. David Sirota, author of *The Enthusiastic Employee: How Companies Profit by Giving Workers What They Want*, says that in companies with high employee morale, stock prices outperformed other companies in the same industries by more than 2 to 1. Companies with low employee morale found their stock prices trailing behind industry competitors by nearly 5 to 1.[28]

Communication is King for High Performers

Having a stable and steady workforce is a first step to an engaged, high-performing organization. While there's no silver bullet, communication is king when it comes to fighting off turnover issues.

A 2009 survey[29] conducted by the Workforce Productivity Group (i4cp) found that internal communications has an effect on staff retention. Eighty-one percent of U.S. respondents named internal communications as their favorite method, and among the higher performers, 91 percent named communication as their top method of minimizing turnover (compared to 71 percent of the lower performers). Talent management and succession planning came in second and third respectively.

Higher-performing organizations are also taking action now and planning for the future to minimize turnover with rewards and training:

- Eighteen percent have already increased compensation levels to reduce turnover (compared to just 7 percent of lower performers), and about the same percentage (18 percent) are planning compensation increases in the next six to 12 months.
- Sixty-six percent are planning leadership training.

As the business environment continues to change at an ever-accelerating pace, leaders are challenged to keep employees focused, committed, and engaged. The good news is effective communication can do just that.

TRY IT TODAY

- Look at your current communications. Are you treating them as a luxury or a necessity?
- Assess your level of engagement. Do you know where your employees stand?
- Communication means business; engaged workforces have better productivity. Do a walkabout. Ask employees what they think is the direction of the company. How do they see their team contributing? How do they "live it" in their daily jobs?

A Leader's Role

"The art of communication is the language of leadership."

*– James Humes, best-selling author
and speechwriter for five U.S. presidents*

Starting thought

A leader is like tofu

The nature of leadership is changing rapidly today. As we work with leaders at all levels, I've seen firsthand that many of them are operating without a clear understanding of the critical competencies needed today to succeed. These skills are different in many ways than skills needed in the past.

As a result, leaders aren't getting the best from their people or themselves, and their organizations are missing out on opportunities. I love what Jim Collins, author of *Good to Great* said: "Good leaders are like tofu: clearly part of the meal, perhaps even the main source of nutrition, but the spice is provided by everyone around them." [30]

Organizations don't inspire employees—leaders do. These leader**communicators** know how to meet employees' communication needs to build trust and credibility. And they ensure their actions match their words. That's what leads to the discretionary effort every leader wants and needs today from his or her team.

Most problems in business today lie in the absence of good communication. Many leaders weren't promoted because of their leadership communication skills. Savvy leaders today know their next success most likely depends on mastering their ability to communicate and connect the dots in new ways.

**What additional skills
do you need to succeed?**

Know Your Role

Whether it's in your detailed job description or not, leaders at every level of an organization have an important and specific role to connect the dots between the big business picture and what it means for employees.

Specifically, the role of a leader is to:

- Seek out and provide **context** for organizational information to ensure your team clearly understands how its priorities and goals fit into the organization's and the workgroup's overall priorities and goals

- Make information **relevant** so every employee understands how he or she fits in

- Provide **job-related information** so your team receives essential information to help them do its job effectively

- Provide **information and feedback on individual performance** and other employee-related matters (e.g., recognition of achievements and contributions)

For leaders, this means:

- Open communication with employees

- Sufficiently informing employees so they:

  - Know and understand the organization and work group's business goals and strategy

  - Understand how the goals and objectives of their work group or team fit into the organization's overall future direction

  - Understand how the organization is performing as well as their business unit's and specific work group's or team's performance

- Encouraging constructive debate

- Encouraging sharing of ideas about important issues facing the organization

- Informing employees of reasons behind the decisions that affect them

- Listening

Strategies for Influence in a Matrix Organization

Many organizations today have matrix reporting structures, which means it's all the more important to exert influence and your leadership impact in a smart way to be able to move people to action.

Use these strategies from best-selling author Patrick Lencioni's book, *"The Five Dysfunctions of a Team,"* to influence people:

1. If you want to change how people behave, first change how they think. Start by identifying what behavior it is that you need to change. Ask yourself: What is it that you need to get done that isn't happening?

2. Think about where your audience is coming from and what their needs and perceptions are. With that in mind, plan your messages so you're answering two important questions in a way your audience can understand: 1) Is this worth it? and 2) Can this actually be done?

3. Bring your messages to life through experience … ideally personal experience (what you know through your areas of expertise and work experience) or through vicarious experience (that is, what you know from others' experience). Use stories to illustrate your points to paint a picture for your audience.

Leadership Is Entirely Personal

As a leader, how do you get people to follow? Work to elicit one of the three emotional responses:

1. The feeling of significance. People want to feel valued and know that they really matter—no matter how they contribute to an organization. Feeling significant leads to loyalty.

2. The feeling of community. Community occurs when people feel a sense of purpose around work and feel part of something larger than them.

3. The feeling of excitement. People want excitement and challenge in their lives. Energy from a leader keeps followers engaged and can inspire them to become leaders.

TIP:
Build trust in three simple steps:

1. Understand every employee's communication needs.

2. Engage in real, two-way dialogue that creates shared meaning.

3. Reinforce words with actions.

Supervisors Need to be Super-Communicators

Even though employees will always want to hear from the top, no one's more influential than an employee's supervisor. Virtually all research shows that a supervisor is the employee's preferred source for job-related information. It's no wonder employees look to supervisors to translate information and make it relevant and meaningful for them.

Supervisors:

- Set the tone and cast a shadow
- Control the flow of information
- Create dialogue (or not)
- Are the central hub of change, quality, efficiency, and innovation

Want to help your supervisors communicate? Train them. It's often easy for senior leaders to talk about the importance of communication; many have professional communicators who provide them with strategy, counsel, and talking points.

For most, communication is a learned skill. Research shows most supervisors don't have a planned approach to communication, despite the amount of time they spend communicating. One of the top barriers to communicating is not knowing how to do it.

TIP:
Phrases to help leaders share what they know

- "I don't know that, but what I can tell you is …"

- "No. Let me explain."

- "That's the way it used to be. Here's what we do now."

- "As I know more, I'll update you."

Middle Managers: You *Are* the Weakest Link

A 2009 survey by The Grossman Group[31] underscores the "frozen middle" that exists in many organizations. Senior leaders are well informed, but there's a significant gap between middle managers and those they supervise.

It's ironic that those who need the most leadership and direction—those at the front lines—are being led in many cases by those who are the least qualified.

According to the national survey of employed adults with supervisors:

- Only half of America's employees (50 percent) agree that their supervisors give them the information they need to do their job well;

- And even fewer employees—four in 10—feel their supervisor keeps them informed about what's going on in the organization (42 percent);

- Finally, only 41 percent of employees feel their supervisor takes action on the ideas and concerns of his or her employees.

Minding the middle is about accountability, training, tools and measurement.

Accountability	**Training**	**Tools**	**Measurement**
Help leaders understand their vital role and hold them accountable.	Provide the training for this learned skill called communication. Teach them how to do it.	Give managers the tools they need to communicate well, and help them use the tools effectively.	What gets measured is what gets done.

What Should Employees Expect of You?

How do you decide what information is mission-critical for employees? Many employees want to know everything that's going on. It's impossible to accomplish and is also an unrealistic expectation.

Follow these two guidelines for when to share (or not share) information:

1. A leader's top priority is sharing information employees need to do their jobs well (work- or job-focused information designed to help employees perform well).

2. A secondary priority is sharing information so employees can advocate on behalf of the organization as brand ambassadors (typically information that builds pride and morale or is important to help get out the organization's story).

Sharing these expectations with staff is critical so they know what to expect from you.

One other key expectation to share with them: if they don't know something or have questions, they need to seek out the information. Communicating is not a spectator sport—it requires active participation. Do your teams understand what you expect from them and what they can expect of you? If not, there's no better time than now to open the dialogue.

TIP:
Sharing information with employees helps them:

1. Know how to do their jobs well and contribute to business results

2. Act as brand ambassadors to tell your organization's story

TRY IT TODAY

- Walk the talk—match your words and actions.

- Effective leadership means connecting the dots for employees. Check for understanding; ask employees to paraphrase what they heard in a conversation or presentation.

- Ask for feedback…and act on it if appropriate (or explain why you can't); employees want to know their input is being heard.

- Communication is a learned skill. Give supervisors the messages, training, and tools they need to connect with their employees and then hold them accountable.

Understanding Your Audience

Starting thought

Banging the drum...repetition means progress

A senior executive once commented to me about the repetition of her messages. "I'm tired of sharing these same messages and stories," she lamented after the umpteenth communication on a crucial topic. *Progress*, I thought.

In a culture of multiple messages, information overload, and often-shifting priorities, I knew we were getting somewhere. We had a core set of messages that we repeated often and in customized ways for multiple audiences. Sure, it was a common sense strategy, but it wasn't common practice (and is often harder than one might think).

How do employees know what's important and what they should pay attention to? Ideally, they hear it from the CEO and their supervisor, they read it in the newspaper, they see it on the intranet or in a blog, and most important, they notice that actions inside the company mirror the words.

Building trust and credibility, and moving people to action, is about consistency of message across touch points that's backed up operationally. Words and actions are aligned. If communication is a key role for supervisors, for example, then they've been told it's their responsibility (words) and are trained, held accountable, and measured regularly on how well they communicate (actions).

This is one of the reasons, by the way, that many supervisors aren't great communicators; they aren't held accountable and have never been trained. Both need to go hand-in-hand for trust to be built. How well do your words match your actions? It's incredibly hard work, but nothing generates the buy-in you want faster. And that means the results you want, too.

What messages do you need to be repeating until well beyond you're tired of saying them?

"Your audience gives you
everything you need."
– Fanny Brice

Get to Know Your Audience

These days, employees are bombarded with so much information that it's hard for them to digest it all. Just because you say something doesn't mean others hear and understand you. And that's the whole point of communication—to create shared understanding and drive people to action.

Understanding your audience is key to moving employees to action. The more you know about them, the better you'll be able to persuade them.

The Eight Key Questions Every Employee Has

It's a leader's ability to anticipate and consistently answer The Eight Key Questions™ that will move employees from being focused on themselves to being focused on their team and organization.

Whether employees ask them or not, the reality is there are several key questions that are on their mind, what I call The Eight Key Questions. These questions are a lot like Maslow's hierarchy of needs: employees' basic needs have to be addressed first.

Employees' core questions are "me-focused" questions that help them understand what's happening around them and what it means to them specifically. One question, for example, is "What's my job?"

When the me-focused questions are answered, employees are able to look beyond themselves and become interested in the "we-focused" questions. A we-focused question, for example, is "What's our business strategy?"

It's important to remember that these are questions that employees think about—and perhaps ask—every day…whether they're new to the organization or veterans. The answers may change just as often, too. When change happens—as it often does in today's fast-paced business world—employees immediately go back to the me-focused questions.

THE **EIGHT KEY**
QUESTIONS **?**
A L L   E M P L O Y E E S   H A V E

8. How can I help? ⎤

7. What's our vision and values?

⎸—we

6. How are we doing?

5. What's our business strategy? ⎦

4. What's going on? ————————————— transition

3. Does anyone care about me? ⎤

2. How am I doing?   ⎸—me

1. What's my job? ⎦

© 2000 The Grossman Group
Adapted, with permission, from the original copyrighted work of Roger D'Aprix; all rights reserved

Research also shows that leaders who meet their employees' strategic communication needs don't need to be the most stellar presenters or best listeners. When their intangible needs are met, employees cut leaders slack. Remember that engagement is a gift an employee gives to an organization, and it can be freely given or withheld at any time. These aren't one-time questions that new hires will ask when they start their job. These are the questions employees are thinking about every minute of every day.

When change happens—as it often does in today's fast-paced business world—employees immediately go back to how the change affects them. The challenge and opportunity for leaders is to move them beyond themselves to thinking about the organization again. No small task, but the rewards through increased engagement are significant.

Q. **What is your employees' responsibility when it comes to communication?**

A. We often forget to share our expectations with employees when it comes to communication.

Since communication is a two-way street, employees play as critical a role as leaders. When employees have a question, they need to ask it. If they don't know certain information they need to do their jobs, they need to seek it out. As leaders, we need to remind them of these expectations. Getting to shared meaning means both players—the leader and the employees—play an active role.

Have you shared your expectations with your employees, what you expect of them and, in turn, what they can expect of you? Take a moment to cover expectations the next time your team is together.

A Strategy Fit for a Champion (and the Rest of Us, Too)

Need to garner that must-have support for your initiative? Look to one of the most commonly overlooked audiences—key influencers (the "movers and shakers" from whom others take their cues) and engage them to be your champions.

They can help you raise awareness about a business priority, build support throughout the organization, and communicate key messages—the why, what, how, and what's next—to a broader internal audience.

But first, you need to identify them and convince them. Influencers can help you substantially accelerate the progress of your initiative, or easily get in your way and put a halt to your efforts. Look at influencers as your potentially toughest, but one of the most critical, audiences. If you can convince them, your initiative is bound to succeed because they're your first litmus test; they're going to ask the tough questions they know others will ask. After all, their credibility and reputation (not to mention influence) are on the line.

For the best results, ensure you select champions wisely, seek their input, train them, and then equip them with core communications tools they can use to dialogue with their peers and other audiences. Useful tools might include a master presentation, a one-page visual executive summary, and a frequently asked questions guide.

TIP:
Take a minute to do a quick mindset analysis before presenting to an audience:

- Where is the audience coming from?
- What are their positive or negative perceptions?
- What are they concerned about?

Then, ensure you present with their needs in mind. The more you know about your audience—whether a group of employees or a senior executive—the better able you are to persuade them.

The Big "Oops:" Communication Mistakes that Can Shut Down Employees (Literally and Figuratively)

Context and relevance. They're two of the most important concepts for a leader in communicating effectively with employees. Put this communication in the larger context and help me understand what it means to me. The appropriate context and relevance will accelerate understanding and engagement.

When you ask employees what gets in the way of their understanding, here are the most common communication mistakes:

- Inconsistent messages
- Talking at employees instead of with them
- Communication delays; not responding quickly while waiting for "all" the information
- "Spinning" messages instead of speaking truthfully
- Not telling the truth or keeping silent
- Using language employees don't understand
- Relying on technology that breaks down or others don't have

TRY IT TODAY

- Align your words and actions to build trust and credibility. Regularly check to ensure you are anticipating and consistently answering The Eight Key Questions all employees have.

- Enlist your champions. Think about the key influencers in your organization and how they can help you with a current or future communications initiative.

- Know your audience and tailor your communication to their needs. When planning your next communication, take a minute to do an audience mindset analysis.

Building Trust

Starting thought

Want trusting employees? Focus on actions not words.

Talk is cheap. Especially when it comes to leaders and their ability to build and maintain trust. Just ask any employee. To them, it's actions and results that matter most. It's hard to escape newspaper headlines that chronicle the latest corporate scandal, reminding us of the disastrous consequences when the actions of corporate leaders don't match their words.

Today, employees are putting company leaders of all levels on notice that when it comes to earning trust, they better work a little harder. Trust is elusive. It takes a lot of hard work to earn but very little effort to lose. Maintaining it takes conscious effort and skill. Once lost, trust can be nearly impossible to get back. Yet, employees who trust their leaders are far more likely to be engaged in achieving results.

In the graduate course I teach at Columbia University, my students thirst for practical ideas and insights on ways to build trust. The burning question I often hear from my graduate students and many senior executives is, how can I get employees to trust me? We're not talking about merely managing reputation. This is about creating a deep bond of believability between executive and manager, superior and subordinate, that motivates employees to put forth the effort needed to make their organization successful.

Doing this well requires a new set of skills. It's the evolution of communications as a leadership responsibility. leader**communicators** recognize that to truly inspire employees to create a better future, and for them to believe in that future, employees must trust the person telling them what to do.

leader**communicators** also recognize that you can't simply say and do the right things once in a while. They consistently deliver the same messages and actions across all of their business relationships, because they know that trust is earned when their actions match their words. They also understand that trusting employees are more likely to project a positive external company image that fosters customer loyalty and trust.

What are you doing to earn your employees trust?

"Trust has to be earned, and should come only after the passage of time."

– *Arthur Ashe*

Greater Trust Improves Productivity

Building trust is not a soft business issue. Greater trust in leaders benefits the bottom line and your employees' well-being. What we know intuitively has been proven in a study on happiness and well-being: relationships are more related to happiness and satisfaction than material wealth, and these relationships affect productivity in the workplace and the bottom line.

"We overstate the importance of material consumption," said John F. Helliwell, a fellow at the University of British Columbia's Canadian Institute for Advanced Research, who surveyed more than 100,000 people worldwide on the value of people's social connectedness through their networks and engagement in the community around them.[32]

Helliwell assigned dollar figures to recognizable values to show how important certain factors are to well-being. People value being part of an organization at the equivalent of around $25,000; seeing family and friends frequently is valued at four to five times more than that. Folks surveyed gave a negative value to being away from their spouse, and illness topped the list of negative factors.

At work, the most valuable factor of well-being was trust toward management, valued at more than $500,000. These results reinforce for leader**communicators** what's truly important as a leader.

Yes, having the technical and management skills is how you won the job. But how you win the commitment of your people is by being worthy of their trust. After all, people don't work for companies; they work for people. And they work best for leaders who have earned their trust by behaving authentically against a set of values and guiding principles.

Check out the list at right to see how many of these trust-building characteristics fit your leadership style. Then focus on the weak spots and start building trust today!

Building trust that lasts

When people trust you, your ability to persuade them is increased tenfold. Here are tried-and-true strategies that work:

- Be approachable and friendly (people trust leaders they like)
- Balance the need for results with being considerate of others and their feelings
- Instead of using your position power, work hard to win over people
- Ensure your words and your actions match
- Actively listen and check for understanding by paraphrasing what you've heard
- Show support for your team members, even when mistakes are made
- Be honest and tell the truth; telling people what you think they want to hear erodes trust

As leaders, we can't underestimate the power of the shadow we cast and, subsequently, our ability to influence behaviors to drive results. It's not enough to engage employees in driving the business strategy, we need to demonstrate visibly what it looks like. No one is more influential than leaders. What behaviors are you trying to drive today?

Engaged Employees …

- Are more satisfied, committed, and loyal
- Work harder
- Reduce costs
- Create more satisfied customers
- Are less likely to be absent or leave
- Put in extra time, brainpower, and energy
- Adapt more quickly to change

Factors That Hinder Engagement

- Complex business environment
- Constant change
- Competition in the marketplace
- The push to do more with less
- Information overload
- Conflicting agendas
- Job insecurity
- Disconnect between what leaders say and do
- Balance between work and family

According to research, **55 percent** of employees say what leaders say and do has the most impact on their perception of an organization.[33]

Whether People Trust You Is Completely Up to You

Author Stephen Covey defines trust in a simple and clear way—the "confidence born of two dimensions: character and competence." He describes having low trust as a "hidden tax" on every interaction and transaction, which gets in the way of results and raises costs.[34]

As a leader, trust starts—or stops—with you. Trust is contagious. When you trust others and demonstrate that you can be trusted, it sets into motion an expectation and opportunity for others to trust and be worthy of trust in return. If you distrust, then others will.

This plays out in every day scenarios that can build others' trust in you and ultimately elevate your impact:

- When you collaborate with others across teams and functions (and avoid silos and turf battles), you signal to your team to do the same and work will get done better and faster (not to mention more peacefully).
- When you keep your promises—whether seemingly significant or small—others will, too.
- When you give credit when others do great work, they'll appreciate you for it and follow suit.
- When you admit that things went wrong or didn't turn out as you had planned, they'll see you as accountable, credible and focused on being better—and they'll follow your lead.

One more thing about building trust—it's a lot easier for people to trust you when they know you and see you. There's a saying that the only difference between leaders and Elvis is that Elvis has been spotted. Don't try to lead from behind the desk—it doesn't work. Walk the halls. Have lunch in the lunch room. Keep your door open. Strike up a conversation. Let people see you and get to know them—and let them get to know you.

TRY IT TODAY

- Employees who trust their leaders are far more likely to be engaged in achieving business results. Talk with your leadership teams about how trust and engagement affect productivity in the workplace and the bottom line.
- Build trust by linking your communication messages to practical ideas and insights.
- Review The Eight Key Questions all employees have *(chapter 3)* to gauge how well you and your organization are meeting employees' communication needs.

Focusing on Fundamentals

Starting thought

Take an about face: join my anti-social media club

I often get asked about what I'm seeing in the communication industry and where we're headed. And I've been getting a lot of questions these days about social media on the inside of organizations. A good friend of mine calls himself the anti-social social worker, so I'm unofficially dubbing myself the anti-social media guy.

Don't get me wrong. I love technology. Beyond internal communications strategy and execution, The Grossman Group helps organizations think about integrating technology into their internal communications arsenal to move people to action. What we also do is recognize each organization's unique culture and where they fit in the technology spectrum and propose solutions that don't intimidate employees but help to further the business goals.

But what employees want, and in many cases crave, is connection…a real connection to the people around them.

Technology might seem easier, and I'm as mesmerized by it as anyone, but employees today want face-to-face communication—good ol' non-sexy, non-whizbang voice-to-voice or face-to-face conversation. They're confused about where our organizations are going and their role in getting there. They want to hear from their senior leaders more. They have big questions that need to get answered, and they're looking for meaning…not just answers or words. They not only want to understand but want to be inspired, motivated, and engaged. That's where you come in. All of us can start the revolution today.

Join my anti-social media club. Maybe we could call it, "About Face."

> **What strategies are you using to be visible and have real dialogue with your employees?**

"You have to monitor your fundamentals constantly because the only thing that changes will be your attention to them. The fundamentals will never change."

– *Michael Jordan*

Planning Your Communication

Just as you have an ongoing plan for continuous improvement in your business, you should have a plan to continuously improve how you communicate with employees.

As leaders, you set the tone for how information flows, how employees work together, and whether employees talk with each other and with you. Everything you say and do communicates, whether you intend it or not, so planning your communication—and checking that they're working—can be the difference in whether employees choose to follow you.

You can ensure continuous improvement in your communication by applying The Deming Cycle, a common continuous improvement process that began with an industrial production focus, but has been adopted to drive business strategy. It's often found as an underpinning of Six Sigma or Kaizen improvement programs.

PLAN	**DO**	**CHECK**	**ACT**
Establish business and communication objectives and processes to deliver expected results.	Implement new communication processes, often on a small scale, if possible.	Measure new communication processes and compare results against the expected results to discover any differences.	Analyze differences to determine their cause. Apply changes for continuous improvement.

Apply this model repeatedly to achieve your intended business and communication objectives.

The 5 Ws and an H for Communicating Virtually Anything

Ask any journalist and they can tell you about the 5 Ws and an H. Any solid news story covers those six basic ingredients. The same is true for communicating inside an organization.

Want to ensure you don't forget a critical detail in your communications? Think 5 Ws and an H to ensure you're not missing an important detail, sharing the all-important context, and making it relevant for your audience.

What
What's the decision? What does it mean? What should I know? What's in it for me?

Why
Why is it the right decision? Why now? Why is it important?

Who
Who made the decision? Who's in charge? Who does it impact?

Where
Where is this decision coming from? Where/what locations will it affect? Where can I get more information?

When
When is this happening?

How
How was the decision made? How will it be implemented? How will communications flow internally and externally? How does it impact me?

In communicating your message, the order is important. Adult learners want to know the "**what**" first and then the "**why**." The rest can follow logically.

TIP:
Question yourself before you communicate

You might have a sense of what you want to communicate. But before you do, ask yourself two critical foundational questions:

1. What's the business outcome I seek from my communications?

2. Who's my audience, and where are they coming from?

It's one of the most common errors in communication: communicating from your perspective (not the audience's) and not being mindful of what your business goal is. How can you motivate someone if you don't know where they're coming from and what's most meaningful for them? And, if you're not focused on a business outcome, your communications aren't going to help you achieve your goals.

The Five Truths of Two-way Communication

Real conversations are becoming extinct in many organizations today.

We take 30 minutes to write five confusing back-and-forth e-mails but won't take three minutes to pick up the phone for a simple conversation.

Move over technology; make room for meaning. Learn to recognize real two-way communication and what it takes. Don't accept any cheap alternatives. As the saying goes, you get what you pay for.

The truisms about two-way communication:

1. The goal is shared understanding and meaning.
2. Effective communication is a conversation.
3. Shared meaning is often assumed but should be confirmed.
4. Training and skill building improves effectiveness.
5. Active listening is a critical skill, because it helps us derive meaning.

Information vs. Communication

Employee to manager: "I'm starving!" Some food for thought on the difference between information and communication: employees are bombarded with information but starved for meaning.

Communication only occurs when an exchange results in shared meaning. Communication is all about facilitating dialogue. To build a successful team, you need to create a culture where it's safe to dialogue about issues to ensure the smartest decisions possible. Here are some suggestions to consider:

- Ensure you have regularly scheduled opportunities to dialogue with your work group, in smaller teams, and with individuals.

- Engage people openly and fully by asking open-ended questions: "What do you think?" "How do you react to that?"

- Listen to what employees have to say and paraphrase to ensure you understand their comment.

- Listen for various points of view and encourage others to express them: "The fact that you and I disagree on an issue is a good thing."

- Listen more than you talk if you want to know what's in your people's heads.

- When asking for input, be prepared to act on it. Otherwise, employees will be less likely to give you input in the future.

Back to School

The next time you're listening to an employee, think to yourself, *Teach me*. It'll arouse your curiosity and make you more open to learning. Plus, you'll listen more and speak less.

Everything you do communicates. Whether you mean it or not, your tone, attitude, and body language say as much as your words. Your staff will listen to what you're saying, but they'll pay even closer attention to what you're doing. That's because actions speak louder than words.

Want to send a message that you're open and available to speak with staff? Keep your office door open, walk the floors, have coffee or lunch with staff. Want your staff to know you were listening to them? Stop talking and really listen. Play back what they tell you, so they know you heard them loud and clear. Want your staff to follow certain procedures? Lead by example, following those same procedures.

They'll know what's important to you and what's expected of them based on your actions. Imagine that there's a mirror that's always in front of you. Be a good example; model the behaviors you want others to have.

The Truth About Honesty

Don't begin statements with, "To be honest," "Truthfully," or "Honestly."

That always makes me wonder whether the person wasn't being honest before.

Just tell the truth and get on with it. That's one relationship-building step you can use with anyone, anytime.

Always Start at Chapter 1: Become a Pro with Context

Context literally means, "to weave together." One of the most important jobs of a leader is to provide context (the other is to ensure relevance). Context makes everything else make sense.

Always begin communication with chapter one. It's "once upon a time" in headline form, and it starts at the very beginning of the story you're trying to tell. Set up the situation and show the big picture, so everyone starts with the same base of knowledge. Chances are, we might be on chapter three of the story but need to remember that our staff is most likely starting at the very beginning.

Another way to think about context is a map at a large airport. To understand "where you are," you need the big picture. That's the context. Then you can determine where you want to go and how you might get there.

Active Listening is as Easy as 1-2-3

1.

Ask broad, probing, open-ended questions, which allow the listener to take the conversation in a direction they choose:

- "Help me understand."
- "How do you envision…?"
- "What other strategic alternatives did you consider?"

2.

Ask more directive questions, which focus the conversation and get at additional specifics:

- "Tell me more about…?"
- "How would this work?"
- "How did you come to this conclusion?"

3.

Summarize what you're hearing and check for understanding

- "So, if I'm understanding you,…"
- "Tell me if this is what you're saying,…"

The Top Seven Strategies for Being a Better Listener

- Stop talking.
- Suppress the inclination to think about what you are going to say next.
- Don't multitask; focus on the speaker closely.
- Ask questions to ensure you understand.
- Paraphrase back what you're hearing.
- Listen with an open mind, not for what you want to hear.
- Pay attention to what might not be said.

The "I"s Have It

When coaching or giving tough feedback, "you" statements can often put the listeners on the defensive: "You shouldn't have…"

Instead, talk about yourself from an "I" perspective, using what's often called "I statements." When you talk about yourself, you're able to better express genuine thoughts and feelings and maintain a respectful attitude. You also take personal responsibility. For example:

- "I've noticed…"
- "When you do this, I feel…"
- "I find it difficult…"

Correctly used, I statements can be part of trusting and valuing both yourself and the other person.

Difficult Messages Made Easy

Having tough conversations is just that—tough. It's challenging for many of us, but it is a critical skill for any leader's toolbox.

Addressing issues up front with your team keeps everyday speed bumps from mushrooming into larger problems. You'll establish yourself as a person who takes tough situations and transforms them into opportunities for building trust and honest, open relationships. The better prepared you are, the smoother it will go and the better your chances are of achieving your desired outcome.

Follow these six steps to prepare for a tough conversation:

1. **Identify the problem**—For example, business results are not where they should be, staffing changes need to be made, undesired behaviors need to change, etc.

2. **Identify your desired outcome**—For example, put business news in context for employees, inform your team about changes, discuss change toward desired behaviors, etc.

3. **Identify your audience**—Do you need to inform your entire staff? Is it a small group of employees? Is it one employee? Should they all hear the message at the same time?

4. **Structure your key messages/conversation:**

   - Think about your audience's mindset.

   - What do you want your audience(s) to think, feel, and/or do?

   - What will you say (in a calm, constructive way to employees so they understand the situation and your concern)?

     – Consider how to start the conversation.

     – Have stories or examples to share to illustrate your main point.

     – Outline specific actions being taken, and/or that your employee(s) need to take.

     – Identify the questions you will ask (to seek input, check for understanding). For example, "Tell me how you feel about what I just said."

5. **Consider how you will say your message**—Select the right time and place to have a conversation without distraction and with privacy.

- Encourage dialogue so you can get real-time insight on how the employees are receiving the information, what's on their minds, and if they understand what you're saying.

6. **Follow up**—Do your employees have questions? What's on their minds?

It's okay to be human when having difficult conversations. Acknowledge that having to share tough news is hard for you, but also let employees know it's important to you that they know what's going on and that they hear it from you. Employees may not like what you have to say, but they'll respect you for how you say it.

TRY IT TODAY

- Start with the end in mind. Ask yourself, "What's the business outcome I seek from my communication? What's my audience's perspective and needs?"

- Have a plan when you communicate.

- Create real connections with face-to-face communications. Put down your smartphone and go talk to the person you were going to e-mail, or pick up the phone.

- Create a two-way dialogue with active listening. Practice using:
  - Broad, open-ended questions
  - Directive questions
  - A check for understanding

Your Secret Weapon

The *leader***communicator**
Platform

Starting thought

What got you here might not take you there

I remember the day well. I began working with a leader who was promoted to join the senior management team and had taken on significant new responsibilities. This was an incredibly smart, capable, and deserving leader.

As we were talking about his new position, I shared with him what I've learned from working with other leaders in the same situation who, with the best intentions, pushed forward without considering some of the new skills needed to succeed in this transition. "I'm ready," he said. "After all, management wouldn't have picked me if they didn't think I was ready." His confidence had always served him well.

"It's not about readiness," I told him. "It's about new approaches that are critical at this stage of your career. Much of what worked for you in the past will still work well, but there is a whole new set of skills few people anticipate. This is going to provide a new level of development for you."

He had a compelling vision but had never been called on to translate that vision to as many people in as many disparate places in his organization. He struggled with developing and articulating strategy, which is one of the most common challenges faced by senior leaders. He was good at motivating people but not at inspiring them. He was cognizant of making his words and actions match but had never been in a position to impact the overall results of the organization and the livelihood of employees. He wasn't used to the fact that people were watching his every move and analyzing his every word.

It's a truism that leaders don't hear what they're not ready to hear. I suggested we create a leadership platform for him. "Don't need it," he said.

Fast-forward six months. "Remember that conversation we had?" he asked me, catching me in the hallway. "I wasn't open to your perspective, and now I am."

While it felt great to hear that, it would have been even better to help him avoid some of the natural pitfalls he's faced the past six months. We completed a message platform for him, which helped him articulate his strategy, share compelling stories, and ensure his actions match his words.

What counsel are you getting today that you might need to be more open to?

The Tool Few Leaders Have and Every Leader Needs

You don't need to be a politician to have a messaging platform or "stump speech"—every leader should have one. It's one of the must-have tools in your leadership arsenal.

A platform is based on your goals and contains the messages you want to get across every day with various audiences—your boss, the senior management team, your employees, and even the media.

Your message platform should encompass the most credible and compelling ways to talk about:

- Who you are and what you're about (even more important than what you have to say)

- The goals for your team, the behaviors needed, and what you expect

- What your team can expect from you

- How you plan to achieve your team's goals together

- The successes you're realizing

- Most important, stories and anecdotes that bring these messages to life and create an emotional connection with your listener; these messages form the basis of all your communications—every day in every way

TIP:
Paint a picture of a new future or deliver difficult messages with:

- Clarity

- Courage

- Compassion and care

- Conversation

The Thirteen Questions You Must Be Able to Answer

The best leadership platform brings out and leverages your personal strengths, style, and aspirations through authentic communication about who you are and your business priorities.

Employees want a leader who's real and is aware of (and honest about) his or her strengths and weaknesses. They don't want a leader who's like a Hollywood movie set—well-packaged on the outside with nothing behind it. Inspiring employees and engaging them is about meeting their strategic communication needs.

Here are the most common questions employees have for their leaders, which should form the basis of a leader's platform of core messages and actions.

The Top Thirteen Questions for Leaders

1. How did you get to where you are?
2. How do you want people to know you? What makes you tick?
3. What are your expectations of employees?
4. What should they expect of you?
5. On what do you want to put a stake in the ground?
6. What's your vision? Why should various audiences believe in you and the vision?
7. Who are we and what do we do?
8. What are our business goals? Business strategies?
9. What initiatives will drive the business today? In the future?
10. What are the new behaviors you expect employees to perform successfully to achieve your results? How will we get the results needed?
11. What does success look like?
12. How will we measure success?
13. What needs to change to make this happen?

Free to Be You and Me

When you ask employees, they want to be able to connect with their leader—today more than ever before. Employees want to know what you have to say; they also want to know what you stand for.

- Authenticity starts with self-awareness. You need to know yourself and be comfortable sharing who you are with your employees. Employees want to get to know the real you.

    - Who are you as a leader?

    - What motivates you to lead?

    - What were defining moments in your career that helped shape you as a leader?

- Tell stories about yourself that have a clear business moral, allowing your staff to learn something about you as well as what's important to you.

- Communicate similarly when you have bad news as when you have good news. Addressing challenges forthrightly is a credibility-booster for you.

- Develop a message platform to help you tell your story—both your personal and business story.

TRY IT TODAY

- Consider what you might need to be more open to. Think about the last counsel you dismissed; could it have served you well?

- Let your employees know what you stand for. Be authentic. Think about how you'll answer The Thirteen Questions employees have of you.

- Focus on clarity, courage, compassion, care, and conversation next time you have to deliver tough news.

- Have a message platform that articulates your strategy and connects you to your team.

Messaging

*Moving From
Information to Inspiration*

Starting thought

Steve Jobs' Legacy and the Value of Creating a Legacy Statement

While few leaders will rival the likes of Steve Jobs, there's much we can learn from him, and what he did well, especially when it comes to envisioning the future and motivating others to see and achieve what's possible.

Here's what *USA Today* had to say about Jobs:

"Jobs touched lives by shaping our digital universe. He leaned on others for technology, but it was Jobs who dreamed what was possible and had the skill and acumen to deliver products that showed us new ways of thinking."

Quite a powerful legacy.

I wonder whether Jobs purposefully thought about his legacy and what he wanted it to be. How he wanted to be described. I imagine he did.

I'm fortunate to work with many senior leaders and help them develop and articulate their aspirations for the future. With many, we talk about the legacy they want to achieve. Some aren't open to the topic, saying their legacy will be determined by outside factors; for others, it's the start of a powerful dialogue that sets in motion a paradigm-shift about one's work, career, and life.

Creating a legacy strategy and statement can seem daunting at first, yet paves the way for a different kind of strategic focus and passion. It's the perfect complement to your business goals and strategy, and can help guide not only your thinking, but more importantly, your behaviors and the behaviors of others.

More than just how you will be remembered, a legacy strategy and statement help you purposefully plan and guide your own future as you think about what you're uniquely qualified to do for your organization. It'll help you create your future. And might even make for a great mention in a *USA Today* article.

How might creating a legacy statement benefit you?

"You can have brilliant ideas, but if you can't get them across, your ideas won't get you anywhere."

– Lee Iacocca

Imagine Statements

"I envision." Those two words can potentially change your life, the lives of your employees, and help you get better business results.

It's about your dreams, aspirations, and the future you envision. One of the most critical skills of best-in-class leaders is an ability to paint a picture of the future. It's not just any future but one that each of us can envision…that inspires us…that we want to be a part of. These "dreams" often start with the words "imagine" or "what if."

State your business goal and then talk about what's possible. Employees want to be engaged in a meaningful journey toward a worthy destination. That dream sets the context and playing field and describes where you're headed.

TIP:
What makes a good "imagine" statement? It should:

- Tie to your goals

- Describe a compelling image of what's possible and what you're trying to create

- Appeal to others to share in the future you envision

- Show others how they benefit; in the end, it's an inspirational future that people want to be a part of and will work hard to help you get there

Develop Your Messages with the Audience in Mind

Messages will best resonate with your audiences if you first think about where they're coming from and their current mindset.

- What do they already know?
- What are their concerns?
- What are their positive perceptions or assets to leverage?
- What do they want to know?
- How do they want to know it?

Key messages are only words on paper until they spark action. Moving your audience to action is about influencing how they think and feel. An individual's thoughts impact how he or she feels, which impacts what he or she does.

TIP:
Before creating messages, ask yourself:

- What does my audience already know?
- What are their positive and negative mindsets?
- What do I want my audience to think? feel? do?

Think. Feel. Do.

Creating an emotional connection is the fastest way to move someone to action. What do you want your audience to *think*? How do you want your audience to *feel*? What do you want your audience to *do*?

What? That's Where You Start

In communicating virtually any message, you always need to start with the what—what's happening?

Don't assume people know. Set the stage and give the big picture first.

Then, cover the why. Explain the rationale.

Next is the how and when—how will this impact our team, the organization, and most important, the employee? When will this change take place?

Last, check for understanding by asking questions and soliciting feedback. That's how you reach a shared understanding. Otherwise, you haven't communicated.

Get Your Point Across in 15 Seconds or Less

What's your 15-second elevator speech? Here is how to tell your story quickly and effectively.

- Grab attention from the start, so your listener wants to hear more (skip the jokes!).
- Convince your listener of what's in it for him or her, speaking in terms he or she can relate to.
- Set the stage for follow-up...and stay committed to it.
- Communicate with passion, knowing you may never have this opportunity again.
- Summarize your key points.

Don't miss the chance for a great conversation, which starts with a great elevator speech.

Make the Communication Vacuum Work for You

The "communication vacuum" fills whether you want it to or not. Some call it the grapevine; others call it hearsay. No matter what you call it, it can be problematic and distracting.

If you aren't talking proactively about issues that are important to your employees, chances are that someone else is. Use the vacuum to your advantage. Get your messages out first. In almost all cases, you know more than you think. You may not have all the answers (you never will!), but you have enough information to let employees know what you know.

You'll get credit for proactively communicating and won't spend valuable time cleaning up the "dirt" in the vacuum.

The key is developing messages based on your audience's needs and then communicating them in multiple ways. Engage key influencers and thought leaders, who typically feed and influence the grapevine the most, along with supervisors throughout the organization. When employees hear the same messages from their supervisor (always their preferred source), from the CEO, read it on the intranet, and hear it through the grapevine, they're more likely to believe it and, most important, act on it.

In fact, one of our clients has a publication called The Straight Scoop—just one of the ways they're addressing the grapevine head-on. In the end, the grapevine can be a powerful resource if you tap it strategically and with discipline.

TRY IT TODAY

- Always communicate with your audience in mind. Before creating messages, write down what you want employees to think, feel, and do as a result of hearing the message.

- Blend vision with reality in order to build trust and credibility. Paint a picture of what's possible for employees so they're engaged in the journey to success.

- Communication will happen with or without you. What's something you're not talking about that your employees are? Make sure your messages are consistent across the vehicles that touch employees.

What's Your Story?

The Power of Storytelling

Starting thought

What's the story with stories?

We all tell stories naturally that illustrate who we are as a person, what we do, and what we believe in. Think of your last conversation with a friend, someone in your family, or a neighbor at a barbecue. "Once upon a time" is an everyday, multiple-times-a-day occurrence.

Yet at work, something happens when we "badge in" at our organizations. Stories get lost, and pie charts and copy-heavy slides take over.

We follow leaders because of how they make us feel. And stories are the most powerful way leaders have of making an emotional connection with employees.

Forget facts. Skip the supporting points. Push past the proof points. Stories rule.

This is especially true in many organizations where the majority of employees are left-brained, appreciate the literal, and value a logical sequence of facts. In these cultures, leaders aren't hardwired to share personal experiences, yet stories get the results other communications can't.

How powerful would it be if all leaders had a personalized storytelling platform with a library of stories that tie to the actions they need to accomplish? This platform will help the leader find and raise his or her voice and drive the business results he or she wants.

In today's tough economy, it's the ultimate low-cost, high-return strategy. Isn't that what happily ever after is all about?

> ## Do you have a core set of stories in your communication toolbox?

"Their story, yours and mine—it's what
we all carry with us on this trip we take,
and we owe it to each other to respect
our stories and learn from them."

– *William Carlos Williams*

That Reminds Me of a Story

What's the most powerful form of evidence you have when making a business case or trying to persuade?

a) Clear, concise and credible messages

b) Data to back up your messages

c) A great story

d) All of the above

While having all of the above is ideal, the quickest answer is c. Research shows that a great story alone goes a long way, because it's memorable and helps create an emotional connection with the listener.

Stories are powerful tools in any leader's arsenal because they:

- Inspire, galvanize, and engage

- Illustrate rather than assert—stories get the connections and results that abstract communication can't

- Can reach many people quickly and can be easily retold to broaden the audience even further

- Create a sense of membership and unity through shared meaning

- Have a moral or purpose

An effective story should be:

- Simple, easy to tell, and easy to remember

- Short and to the point—the average person's attention span is only about eight seconds

- Purposeful and honest—position the problems on the foreground and then show how they were overcome

- Repeated—keep telling your story until everyone is telling it

Remember, a picture is worth a thousand words, and a story is worth a thousand pictures.

TIP:

Think about what you want your story to do:

- Spark action
- Communicate who you are
- Communicate who the company is
- Foster collaboration
- Share knowledge

Stories as Easy as 1-2-3

Want to create an emotional connection with your employees? Tell a story. Stories instantly capture attention and tap our feelings. What we feel impacts what we do, so stories can be a great way to move employees to action.

Think about a fairy tale:

- "Once upon a time:" introduce what the story is going to be about and an obstacle

- "Here's what happened:" talk about how the characters deal with their challenge

- "Happily ever after:" bring the story to conclusion and share the moral; be explicit about the message or lesson you want people to take away

The End of the Story...Keeping Focused on the Outcome to Drive Results

Like any good communication, stories should have a purpose and tie directly to the end result you're trying to achieve. Here are some tips to keep your stories focused on the outcome so your communications hit their mark:

- Think first of what you want your audience to think, feel, and do and then craft your story to tie directly to the actions and behaviors you're trying to drive.

- Use simple, concise language your audience can understand and react to.

- Choose your words carefully to differentiate your story so it complements the other messages in your presentation.

- Develop a customized repertoire of stories so that you have various personal stories for different messages you want to communicate.

TIP:
Here are some sample story plots to consider:

- Pursuit
- Rescue
- Underdog
- Transformation
- Sacrifice
- Quest
- Discovery
- Lessons learned
- Overcoming obstacles
- Taking charge/leading

"Stories are the creative conversion of life itself into a more powerful, clearer, more meaningful experience. They are the currency of human contact."

– Robert McKee, director and storytelling expert and teacher

TRY IT TODAY

- Stories are the most powerful way to present a business case. Think of examples in your personal or professional life that illustrate an action or behavior you're trying to drive among employees.

- Build your own repository of consistent and relevant stories. Create your story using four simple elements:
    - What was the situation? (content)
    - Who was involved? (characters)
    - What was unique about it? (conflict)
    - Why is this information valuable? (moral)

Managing Change

Starting thought

Tumultuous times call for increased levels of communication and courage

In times of change or uncertainty, organizations need leadership more than ever. That means the quality and amount of communications need to increase. I used to work for a manager who said, "Lead, follow, or get out of the way." Times of change are a litmus test for leadership, which means sharing with employees what we know and what we don't know. This is the time for courageous conversations and straightforward communication. This is the time to talk about how our organizations are well positioned for the future and/or how we're making changes to set ourselves up for future success. Most important, this is the time to share with employees what we need from them.

Clearly, no one has all the answers. But most of us have information and perspective that will be of tremendous value to employees. We'll never have all the answers, and if we wait, someone is going to speak for us and fill the information vacuum. Then, we have to clean up those toxic messages, and our work is doubly difficult.

Guess who's not talking? A survey by Weber Shandwick[35] showed that more than half of working Americans said their employers have not addressed their concerns about the impact of the current economic turmoil. And, although 54 percent said their company leaders have stayed mum on the impact of the financial turmoil, nearly three-quarters said their colleagues are discussing the possibilities.

In some ways, this may be even worse than saying "no comment" externally. When they're cut off from the big picture, employees presume guilt, even in cultures where there's a tremendous sense of pride and a hearty helping of trust.

What's more, talking about the state of our business today makes good business sense. This crisis of confidence has the potential to interrupt the focus on engagement and business results. And worst case, it will become a significant distraction at a time when a steady hand at the wheel is needed. Now more than ever, we need employees to stay focused. But they can only do this with the right direction and information from their leaders.

Clearly, how leaders handle uncertain times will make the difference between winning trust and meeting goals, or backtracking on hard-earned business results and repairing internal reputation.

> How are the quality and quantity of your communications changing during times of uncertainty?

"Be the change you want to see in the world."

– *Mahatma Gandhi*

Change Gridlock

Are your employees feeling stymied by change? Here's a great way to communicate during times of change.

Employees want to know what you know today and understand when you don't have all the facts or details. When you ask employees about their needs, they tell you they want to be kept in the loop as plans develop. Resist the urge to wait until you have all the information to communicate. Chances are, you know a number of key facts that would be helpful for employees to know—and will stop them from filling the information vacuum themselves with misinformation.

Instead, build trust and credibility by communicating regularly on four key topics:

- What we know
- What we don't know
- What we're working on figuring out
- Myths and the facts

These four key topics will help you meet employees' strategic communication needs and keep them engaged as organizations continue to evolve.

Change the Way You Talk about Things, and the Things You Talk about Will Change

You often can resolve a negative situation by changing the context and your delivery. Your words and actions set the tone for those who follow you and your lead:

- Paint the picture of what's possible: help people imagine and live the success you're aiming for.
- Think about the way you have been talking about a major initiative or project. Is it positive? Hopeful? Filled with energy? Cautious? Fearful? Doubtful? Rethink your delivery to inspire and uplift your team.
- Are you celebrating the early wins and successes?

If your approach to discussing business results leaves people feeling less than enthused, change your approach to a team-inspiring one, and watch the results change.

Initiative Indigestion Creates Resistance to Change

We all know that change is part of business and isn't going away any time soon. Employees are bombarded with so much information of all kinds that they can't digest it.

Place change in context to help employees adjust to it:

- Plan your communication at the same time as you plan your change initiative.
- Think ahead and draw clear linkages between the initiative and the business imperative driving the change.
- Make sure employees see the bigger picture and understand the "whats" as well as the "whys."
- Give people a picture of what the change means to them sooner rather than later.
- Create your own calendar of communication events and milestones to ensure you keep people in the loop along the way.

Expressing Disagreement Without Being Disagreeable

When you need to provide criticism, begin by acknowledging the positive points. Then, be specific about what you disagree with. To keep the dialogue open, here are some tips to keep in mind:

- Speak for yourself
- Use neutral and/or positive language
- Don't make assumptions
- Stay away from anything that might be considered personal
- Avoid generalizations and absolutes
- Be positive and upbeat

You want your colleague to be open and hear your thoughts, not be defensive. A free exchange of ideas will lead to the best outcome.

TIP:
Going to Extremes

When you're sharing constructive criticism or coaching employees, avoid extremes like always, never, and worst. Sweeping generalizations like these can trigger a defensive posture by the employee.

10 TIPS
for guiding culture change

Set your sights on long-term success, not just quick wins.

Companies—and their employees—are better off when change is positioned as a constant process. Communicate often to ensure employees have a road map of where the company is headed, what has been accomplished, and what's on deck.

Create a team of "change agents."

Engage and partner with key executives to ensure the change program is properly aligned and positioned. When leaders agree on and "walk the talk"—or even better, "talk the walk"—employees are more likely to follow suit.

Ensure leaders are able, ready and accountable.

Demonstrate that leadership is committed to change by asking them to talk about the change with employees. Managers are critical messengers, so help them succeed by giving them the communication training and tools they need to talk with and listen to employees. They should ask questions, understand perceptions and needs, and ensure those perspectives are shared with "corporate" so they are woven into the overall plan.

4.

Listen carefully and respond religiously.

Create informal and formal feedback channels designed to elicit employee views and perceptions of the change effort. Assign responsibility for personal, timely, and transparent responses to employee concerns to demonstrate employee input is valid.

Assess and create communication channels.

Assess existing communication channels and use only what works (based on employee feedback and usage data). Ensure all external messages—what's reported through the media, to analysts, and other third parties— are consistent with the messages delivered to employees. And, make sure employees hear the news first.

5.

6.

Know your employee audience.

If companies want to change behavior in the future, they first need to understand fully what might be impacting employee behavior at present. Research, such as focus groups, is critical to identifying the root issues and better understanding employee mindsets relative to the company's vision and change effort. These insights will help shape a sound communication plan with more potential for real impact and engagement.

One size does not fit all.

Understand and tailor messages to meet the diverse needs of your key audiences, especially employees. Connect with them and you'll be more likely to be heard and understood. Frontline employees are an important bridge to your customers, competitors, and other important audiences. Do they believe in and live the culture? Are they communicating the key messages in a credible way? Are they effective ambassadors for the brand?

7.

Keep it real when developing the employee communications plan.

Identify and appoint a cross-functional and representative work team to help communicators plan, build, and support the employee communications effort. The plan must be specific, pragmatic, and validated by the people responsible for bringing the plan to life. Make it measurable so you can track and celebrate successes.

TIP:
Employees just want to know what you know

Waiting to communicate until you have all the answers is a risky proposition. Employees just want to know what you know—your "take"—and when you'll have the rest of the information. The information vacuum will be filled whether you want it to be or not. Fill it with what you know instead of something that was heard through the grapevine.

To get to the destination, know where you are at all times.

Clear business—and communication—objectives are instrumental in measuring success. Employees are key to knowing if the change is happening and working, so "take their temperature" along the way. Make sure the employee communications activities are held to the same high standards as other corporate functions: it must be measurable and demonstrate a return on investment.

Communications isn't the fix-all.

Time and again, great companies have learned that no matter how good the communication, culture can't change if operating policies and practices aren't in place to support the change effort. Assess what's working, what should be changed, and what can be eliminated for greater acceptance of the change and a more engaged workforce.

TRY IT TODAY

- In times of change, it's important to tell employees what you know, don't know, what you're working on, and myths vs. facts.

- Think about an initiative or issue you need to address. Now, think about how you can frame it more positively. When talking about change, paint the picture of what's possible; help people imagine and live the success you seek.

- Encourage dialogue, not defensiveness. When you need to provide constructive criticism, begin by acknowledging the positive points and then be specific about what you disagree with.

Communication
Vehicles

How to Drive Home Your Message

Starting thought

Dog-gone it! Anyone can become a (pack) leader.

One of my favorite TV shows is Cesar Millan's Dog Whisperer. If you've seen it, you're familiar with the renowned dog expert who "rehabilitates dogs and trains humans." Before you think this starting thought has gone to the dogs, hear me out about what we can learn from Cesar and his approach to changing behavior.

One caveat: While much of behavior is behavior—whether in the animal or human world— there's a critical factor that's not the same in the dog world as with ours. In the wild, pack leaders are born, not made. This is a significant difference. How we as humans lead and communicate, I believe, are learned skills. Dogs don't take classes to become leaders, but more leaders should take classes to become better leader**communicators**.

On to similarities. Critical to Cesar's work is the concept of the pack. We might call it the organizational culture, or the culture of our team. The pack mentality is one of the greatest forces, he says, in shaping behavior. If anything threatens the pack, it threatens each individual dog's harmony. The need to keep the pack stable and running is a powerful motivating force.

It's the same with the culture inside our organizations: the values, behaviors, and daily actions that make up our culture and operating styles. If something's not building the culture we want, it's destroying it. And no one has a greater impact and responsibility to drive the culture and engage our staffs than we do as leaders—pack leaders.

The shadow we cast by our behaviors and actions speaks volumes to what's important. We are the preferred information source for job-related information. We are the central hub for change. We either create dialogue or we don't. That's our role: to lead our teams in co-discovering, understanding, generating insights, and getting to a shared meaning.

I thought I could teach my lovable stray, Sophie, a Belgian Malinois, on my own, without going to obedience school. (My partner, Steve, suggested nicely that the school was actually for me, not Sophie.) "Don't you always say that leaders are made?" he reminded me.

It was I who needed to become the pack leader, and looking back, I learned a ton. Cesar would be proud!

> ## What skill-building could you benefit from that you might unknowingly not be open to?

"Good communication is as stimulating as black coffee, and just as hard to sleep after."

– Anne Morrow Lindbergh

Smart Ways to Choose and Use the Right Vehicle

Today, people are bombarded with information from all directions; so much so, that the messages you send need to be clear, relevant, and easy to digest, or they won't get attention (and will most likely be deleted).

The vehicle you use to deliver the message is equally important. Just as there are specific criteria you consider when selecting the best method of transportation to take on vacation (budget, number of people traveling, amount of time you want to spend in transit), there are certain factors you need to consider when selecting the most appropriate communication vehicle for your message. Keeping in mind your audience, the type of information, and how much of it you need to communicate will help you choose the right vehicle and substantially increase the likelihood that your message will be received, understood, and acted on.

A Huddle a Day Keeps Chaos Away

Looking for a way to bring renewed energy to your team? Keep everyone aligned and focused? Consider a daily huddle, not to be confused with a daily meeting (perish the thought!).

Huddles:

- Are quick
- Are energizing
- Take place at the same time every day
- Last fifteen minutes, and in times of stability, far less

In huddles, everyone stands and must contribute. Your team lists only the highest priorities of the day and then surfaces and solves roadblocks to achieving them. End of huddle.

If your team is remote, hold huddle phone calls at a standing time when everyone can participate. So, if you haven't huddled since your days in high school sports, give it a try. It may just become the most valuable fifteen minutes of your day.

Defining Moment: Create a Common Language and Understanding

A word to the wise: choose your words carefully. The English language is a beautiful thing except when the same words carry multiple meanings to different people…then it's just alphabet soup!

Many words and concepts are commonly used inside organizations that may mean one thing to senior leadership but something entirely different to staff. There could be 100 different ways to interpret what "urgent" means, or 1,000 different ways to define what's a "priority." How about phrases such as "cost cutting" or "improving productivity?"

It's human nature to expect others to use and understand concepts the same way we would, as if each of us were exactly alike. Are your employees completely clear on what you mean?

Here's a strategy that works to check for clarity with concepts that are critical in your organization and team:

- Write down the key terms you use most frequently; think about your team's vision, values, key priorities, and so on.
- In your next staff meeting, ask your team what those words mean to them.
- Achieve alignment among your team.
- After the exercise, have someone create your own dictionary of definitions.

The work and discussion will be worth it, because you'll know your team is literally on the same page.

Meetings and Voicemails and E-mails, Oh My!

We've all got them, but how can we use these omnipresent tools to help us without taking over our lives? Try these tips:

Meetings

- Do a meeting room "productive environment check" for lighting, temperature, food and drink, flipcharts, markers, etc.

- Distribute an agenda in advance with clear outcomes and accountabilities; make sure you stick to it.

- Agree on meeting goals and what you want to accomplish up-front.

- Dedicate meeting time to issues that need input from the team, not for updates or individual issues.

- Respect time allotment and stick to it; if people know you start your meetings on time, they'll rarely be late.

- Before a meeting adjourns, make sure everyone knows their responsibilities/ next steps.

- At the end of the meeting, ask who else needs to know the information that was just discussed; talk about who will say what to whom and when.

- Compile meeting minutes with decisions and new issues and distribute them.

Voicemails

- Determine if voicemail is the best tool for delivering your message. Is it better in e-mail form, or should you speak with the person(s) face to face?

- Think through and jot down what you're going to say before you say it.

- Keep your voicemails short and to the point; don't ramble.

- Use a friendly, pleasant tone and common sense manners.

E-mails

- Determine if e-mail is the best tool for delivering your message. Is it better in another form, or should you speak with the person(s) face to face?

- Don't send unnecessary e-mails; people are nearing e-mail overload.

- Use proper writing guidelines and check for typos.

- Use a friendly, pleasant tone in your writing; the recipient cannot hear your voice or see your face.

- Don't put anything in an e-mail that you wouldn't want to see on the Jumbotron in Times Square or the front page of a newspaper (e-mails live on forever).

A Winning Mindset Helps Frame Any Presentation

Another update presentation to a leadership council or management team? Develop your presentation with this mindset:

- How can you maximize the opportunity you've been given to further your goals and accelerate the progress of your initiative?

- What do you need from this group of key influencers and stakeholders? How might they help you?

- Could this presentation be an opportunity to discuss the current barriers you face, to test some of your core messages, or to ask for perspectives on crucial questions your team is currently wrestling with ("We'd like your input on a few issues our work team has been discussing")?

Making the most of your time begins with the right mindset.

TIP:

Get your advocates lined up in advance; be prepared to ask the audience questions

- Preparing for a big presentation to sell an idea? Get your advocates lined up in advance. Know where they're coming from and understand what issues they have, if any, so you can address them proactively in your presentation.

  Quick pre-meetings with influencers help you get them on board (or at least not block you) as well as help you practice your presentation.

- Be prepared to ask the audience questions...don't just let them ask you questions. That turns a Q&A into a conversation, and you can know where they stand.

Presentation Strategies that Work

The ultimate way to prepare for any presentation

We've all been faced with this situation: you planned a presentation for thirty minutes and are now told, "We're running late—can you do it in ten minutes?" It's a common (and often dreaded) situation but doesn't need to be. The next time you have a presentation, practice in three ways (note: the first step is to actually plan your presentation and then rehearse):

1. Present in the allotted time
2. Give the same presentation in half the time
3. Present it in five minutes. Presenting in less time is more challenging, because you need to maximize every second. You have to be crystal clear on the outcome you seek and what facts you need to share to drive to that outcome. If you can do it in five minutes, how might you create the right opportunities for dialogue if you have fifteen or thirty minutes? Brevity breeds clarity when you plan and rehearse. And the skills you master, once internalized, will get you noticed.

An Idea You'll Flip Over

Have something you want to get your employees' input on? Post a question on a flip chart in your department or office, provide Post-its, and watch the ideas grow. It's an informal focus group of sorts, where employees will periodically revisit the question and ideas, leading to great collaboration in real time (and without meeting!). Working virtually? Create an electronic message board.

With the right open-ended question (e.g., "What ideas do you have for how we can improve _____?"), a ton of potential solutions will result. Chances are, you'll get ideas you never would have thought of. Even better, employees will appreciate being a part of the process.

TRY IT TODAY

- Hold a daily huddle with your team to maintain alignment and focus on key priorities.

- Choose your mode of communication wisely (meetings vs. voicemails vs. e-mails) by considering your audience, the type of information, and how much you need to communicate. Stop before sending an e-mail today and ask yourself, "Is this the best way to deliver my message?"

- Post a question on a flip chart or electronic message board to solicit employee feedback.

CEOs: Avoid These Mistakes and Turn Your Strategy Into a Reality

Starting thought

The mistakes CEOs can't help but make, and the fixes they can't afford not to make

I don't know any senior management team that doesn't spend days, weeks, working tirelessly on their organization's strategic plan.

They review the data, envision the future, and shape it into a cohesive entity that fits on a piece of paper. It's pretty amazing, really. And it's one of the toughest challenges any team faces: to articulate the strategy that's going to get you the results Wall Street and others expect.

So why is so much of that hard work left to chance when it comes to implementation? Think about it. There's inspiration…perspiration…and group conversations throughout the strategic planning process…lots of nodding heads and even a few moments that feel like Kumbaya.

You came out with a clear sense of purpose and mission. You charged your direct reports to communicate the strategy to their teams. Everyone left jazzed about the plan and your overall path forward. Done…right? But is it true alignment…or is it all just an illusion?

I can tell you from too much experience, it's the latter. I've seen this scenario play out time and time again.

The truth is that getting that strategic plan in writing is only the beginning. The real challenge is in getting to the outcome of that strategic plan by activating the strategy inside your organization.

When it comes to bringing strategy to life, we've all made costly (and often the same) mistakes—mistakes that make the difference between good and great. And it happens between confusion, skepticism and complacency…and engagement, efficiency and effectiveness.

> If people don't know where you're going and how they fit in, how will they help you get there?

MISTAKE

You don't have a strategy that's codified *(it's in your head or in a few leaders' heads)*

You might have the most compelling vision for your organization, but if you can't get it out of your head and get others to see it and believe in it, it might as well not even exist.

Just because the strategy makes sense to you doesn't mean it will take only an instant for others to see it like you do.

We often think that others think as we do, that others see the world as we do, but it's more likely that there's a lot of ground to cover between their perspective and yours. Employees come to their jobs with their own context, and it's the leader's job to help them understand the collective context, including how you see the marketplace today, and how that led to your strategy.

According to our research, a majority of employees globally don't understand their company's strategy and, as a consequence, how they fit in. Consider the possibility if even 10 or 20 percent more employees understood their jobs better. What might the impact be on productivity, innovation, or revenue? It's up to you to engage others so they have the same clear picture you do of your strategy and where the business is going. The reality is that some may have small windows into your view of the strategy, but very few have the whole picture like you do. Lift the perspective out of your head and get it into others' so they can own it and help you achieve it.

- Put the strategy on a **simple, single piece of paper**. Let it serve as a strategic framework from which all leaders and employees operate.
- **Share the strategic framework** and ensure your leaders are aligned: give leaders the context behind the strategy so they understand how you got there and ask them to make the strategy relevant for their teams.
- Use the strategic framework consistently in your communications with employees so it becomes familiar to them and they **see what's happening and how it ties to the strategy** (they know what's important when they see and hear it from multiple sources).
- As your thinking evolves about the strategy (quarterly, annually, etc.), **update your framework** and communicate regularly so employees are in the loop and understand the reasons behind decisions.
- **Celebrate "wins,"** always connecting back to and reinforcing the core elements of the strategy.

MISTAKE

You mistake nodding heads on your leadership team for alignment

There's a bobblehead for everything these days: superheroes, athletes, celebrities, politicians and my new favorite—our Founding Fathers. Nothing says independence like a head-bobbing John Adams.

Unfortunately, there are too many leaders who are bobbleheads, too.

We've all been in those meetings where the leader shares ideas and everyone in the room nods with resounding approval. The senior-most leader leaves the meeting thinking, "Great, everyone's on board and moving full speed ahead." Except what usually happens is people go back to business as usual, or chat up the grapevine about how the ideas discussed will never work. It's time to stop the bobbleheads.

How do you ensure alignment?

- **Engage everyone in the discussion**. Don't allow bobbleheads to speak with their nods. Draw them out to find out what they're thinking.

- **Ask open-ended questions** of your leadership team to get real-time input and commitment. How someone answers a question tells you what they're thinking.

- **Elicit opinions** to ensure diverse perspectives are aired and discussed.

- Once you gain alignment, **ask leaders to share how the strategy is relevant** to their area of the business.

- **Set clear expectations** and accountabilities so every head-nodder has a clear set of actions related to their critical role in activating the strategy.

- **Follow up individually** with your leaders for their perspective on what was discussed. Ask questions to engage each one in dialogue, and check how well a leader is customizing the information for his or her team.

- **Give leaders an assignment**: Have them reach out to their staff and come back to you with perspective on parts of the strategy that seem confusing and/or barriers that may exist to implementing the strategy (along with recommended solutions).

TIP:
In a study of 472 worldwide organizations, only one-third (37 percent) reported their employees were "effectively aligned to the missions and visions of their businesses."[36]

MISTAKE

Elements of your strategy mean different things to different people

When it comes to strategy there are two rules. Rule #1: Have a strategy. Rule #2: Make sure everyone is literally on the same page in understanding the components of the strategy and how to implement it.

All too often, strategies contain words or concepts that take on as many meanings and interpretations as the number of people who read them. Take the word "growth," for example. It's a common term used in just about every strategy (for good reason). But what does growth really mean in your strategy? Is it incremental growth, organic growth, growing the pipeline, growing the global footprint, growing the number of employees, growing through acquisition, or something else?

Your answer will make a difference in how people think about growth, and the actions they take as a result. You want to ensure you're driving the actions you want, which in turn lead to the business outcome you want. Take a cue from the trusted dictionary and literally define what each of the concepts means in your strategy. Share the definitions with your leaders and employees. Take the time for real dialogue with your teams (that way, you'll know if they're on the same page as you or if they need more clarification). Get them to internalize the strategy so they know how it connects to their job.

Define your strategy—literally:

- **Be global**: Ensure the core terms you use will work globally; strip away jargon or buzz words.

- **Be all-encompassing**: Define all the important terms even if they seem obvious to you.

- **Be precise**: Use clear and specific language in defining your terms.

- **Be real**: Describe how you're thinking about the business today and where you want it to go as if you were talking directly to a front-line employee.

- **Be visual**: A picture's worth a thousand words.

I'll never forget a meeting with the top 10 executives of a company. We were there to talk about communicating their new strategy to employees. Part way through the meeting, the CEO realized his own leadership team was defining core elements of the strategy in different ways, including as it applied to the business model, franchising model, and current approach to create loyal customers.

We took a step back and got everyone aligned on the key terms and how to define and talk about their business. It became a defining moment for the leadership team because even the best communication plan can't engage employees if leadership is sending different messages.

MISTAKE

You fail to interpret the outside world *(that's driving your strategy)* for your employees

At the heart of organization-wide alignment is a common context with a focus on the customer. Context influences how we interpret information. It's the lens through which we view and make sense of the world.

Each of us comes to the workplace with our own context because of how we're raised, our experience, background, and so on. That's a wonderful thing because we need diversity more than ever today, especially when innovation is critical for success.

However, to make smart business plans and decisions, employees need to understand the collective context we all agree on as an organization. The goal is one message; many voices. Every leader might have a specific point-of-view on customer issues, the marketplace or top strengths that an organization needs to leverage. In the end, the leadership team needs a collective point-of-view that everyone backs. You don't want a rogue leader confusing employees or causing you or other leaders to do clean-up because they choose to share their individual opinions vs. your collective leadership view. Alignment means getting on the same page—literally.

The biggest benefit of a common context is that your leadership and employees are focused on the customer and not on the navel-gazing that often happens inside organizations.

"Years of success had led us to lose touch with why P&G was in business. Employees had drawn to internal interests. I needed to define the relevant outside, where the results are most meaningful."

– A.G. Lafley, former CEO, P&G [37]

Think of your strategy as a journey.

Before you embark on a journey, there are many considerations and details to plan. The more you prepare and plan, the more enjoyable and fruitful your journey will be.

- **Help employees understand why the journey is a good idea for the company and them as individuals.** Explain the "why" behind a plan or change, including current results, new customer requirements, and recently acquired competitive data that boosts the credibility of the "why."

- **Define the destination.** Get employees excited and help them envision the destination. Articulate the goal with clear performance benchmarks and data.

• **Explain the "how"—or what you expect of
employees.** Help employees to understand their role
in reaching the destination. Detail the behaviors you
seek, and explain how those behaviors will deliver
the desired results. Provide
a road map and explain where
there may be challenges
throughout the journey, but
remind them of the benefits
of reaching the destination.

• **Answer the "what's in it
for me" question that all
employees ask.** They need
to know that the destination
will be as wonderful for them
as it will be for the company
or others within the company.

• **Log the journey.** Solicit feedback
along the way. Listen for the right
messages to be played back to
you so that you feel confident your
employees are on the right path to
the destination. Allow them to ask
questions and seek clarity on why
one road is better than another.

By predicting and answering the **who**, **what**, **when**, **where**, **why** and **how** questions,
you will enable your workforce to understand the context and relevancy of your strategy.
Preparation and detailed communications will help you have a smooth journey and arrive
at your destination on time and ready to enjoy the adventure.

MISTAKE

You don't engage your employees
and extended leadership in the
development of your strategy

Nutritionists today urge parents to engage children in meal preparation because then they'll be more likely to eat healthy food.

By encouraging children to help with the shopping, unpacking the bags, writing the menu and the cooking itself, parents significantly increase the likelihood that a child will be vested in the final outcome and actually *eat the meal*. The same principle applies to the strategy-development process in corporations. All leaders start down the same path to a strategy based on market research and customer preference data, but smart leaders quickly engage layers of leadership and employees throughout strategy conceptualization.

Use these five tips to get your employees on board early and to ensure their participation in the long run:

- **Complete a SWOT analysis.** As part of getting to a shared context, engage your leaders to determine and then synthesize the most important strengths, weaknesses, opportunities, and threats.

- **Develop and then test messages.** Based on the SWOT, work with your leaders to develop or validate/update your vision, mission, values and goals. This comprises the Strategic Frame 1.0. Then test messages with other layers of leadership for their feedback and to identify barriers. Use their input to develop the Strategic Frame 2.0 as part of your iterative message testing. You might use the same strategy with key influencers throughout the organization who will be critical players to activate employees. Their input will help you create the next version of the plan: the Strategic Frame 3.0.

- **Do a reality check.** Ask front-line employees who are the closest to customers how the strategy applies to them. If they can personalize it, and it makes sense to you, the strategy is headed in the right direction.

- **Leave the door open for feedback.** Create a resource for employees to provide ongoing feedback directly to leadership. If their voice matters, they will ultimately use that voice to advocate in the future.

- **Train employees and arm them with the tools they need.** Give employees the opportunity to take ownership of the strategy in a methodical and fun way so that they feel empowered to be the brand ambassador you want them to be. Your goal is to ensure they can articulate how they fit in. If they can do that, they get the strategy and are in the best position to help move the organization forward.

The seed of a strategy idea conceived by a small group of 10 can successfully and rapidly grow throughout a multi-national, multi-million dollar company through systematic employee engagement.

MISTAKE

You need to dress up in disguise and be on a reality TV show to understand your front-line employees

If you feel the only way to really know what's going on at the front lines of your company is to go undercover, there's something wrong. Leaders should not be in the dark about the interface between their front-line employees and customers.

How can you get to know your front-line employees, what motivates them, and how to get them to be highly-valued brand ambassadors?

- **Spend time with employees.** It's a simple theory—and it works. Allocate time each month to walk the halls, eat lunch in the cafeteria, talk face-to-face with the factory manager or employees on the floor. Ensure that on every trip, you allocate time to talk with employees at the location you're visiting. Schedule these activities in your calendar, just like any other critical appointment.

- **Ask questions that connect to the strategy.** For example, "Help me understand how you see the work you're doing contributing to our strategy?"

- **Reinforce what you want to see more of.** Hear a great idea? Recognize it. See someone exhibiting one of your core values? Recognize him or her. Share genuine, appreciative feedback with employees.

- **Provide an avenue to listen regularly.** Use technology appropriately to create channels of communication so that employees can reach out to you when they have a question, concern or idea. Don't commit to this, however, unless you plan to answer the questions or emails yourself. Employees know canned responses or those that don't sound like they're coming from you.

MISTAKE

No data exists on the state of communication and what needs to be improved from employees' perspective

23

30

Leaders are hungry for data to make business decisions on everything from new products and services to whether or not to enter a new market. Yet when it comes to organizational health and employee engagement, many fail to measure what's working and what's not.

Employees can't do their best work and achieve performance goals if they don't understand the strategy...if they're not getting the information they need...if they don't feel like their input is valued.

Since communication is a system, to assess its health you need to understand multiple components, and how they work (or don't work) together:

- Do employees understand the strategy and how their job fits into the overall mission, goals?
- How are the CEO and senior management communicating?
- What is the effectiveness of communication from supervisors?
- How is information flowing (or not)?
- Which messages resonate?
- Which vehicles are most useful?
- Are employees advocating for the organization or not?

Whether measuring your own business unit/function or the overall health of communications inside the organization, leaders (with the help of their communications experts) can make precise decisions about what communications to start, stop or continue to get employees engaged in the strategy and drive performance.

At the end of the day, communication is in the eye of the receiver. Do you know how your employees rate the state of communication in your organization?

TIP:

Employees today:

- Are confused about where their organization is headed
- Want to hear more from senior leaders
- Have questions about overall strategy and how they fit in
- Want to know how they contribute
- Are looking to be inspired

Consider the cost of the following:

- Losing your best employees
- Lack of compliance
- Injuries
- Legal problems
- Unplanned downtime
- Poor procurement processes
- Reduced productivity
- Impaired brand or reputation
- Decrease in employee engagement
- Drops in customer satisfaction

124

MISTAKE

You don't codify your mission-critical information *(into a one-page document)*

Remember travelling in the days before mapquest.com and GPS devices?

Whenever my family would take a road trip, we'd dutifully call the AAA office nearby and request a TripTik, which was a flip book that contained detailed directions that got us from point A to point Z. All the information we needed was there, including the estimated timing for each leg, so we could measure our progress and success.

Most organizations have their own version of a TripTik, and it's usually called the business strategy or strategic direction. But often, it's locked away inside leaders' heads, so the rest of the organization doesn't know when the next turn is coming, how long the trip will take, and, most importantly, what they need to do as individuals and teams to make the journey a success.

Codifying a business strategy into a simple one-page overview is a critical step in creating shared understanding across the entire organization of where the business is headed, why and what everyone needs to do to get there. From there, leaders further down in the organization can customize the strategy depending on their audiences and teams (whether it's by geography, business units, employee levels or other designation) to hone its relevance and ensure the right actions and behaviors.

Make the journey easier for your employees by giving them a simple overview of the business strategy. It will be the definitive road map from which everyone derives their ultimate direction. I often hear leaders exclaim, "Our business strategy is too complicated and sophisticated to put on one sheet of paper!" I usually respond that if they can't summarize the strategy at a high level, how can leaders engage investors, Wall Street, analysts and other key influencers, let alone the employees who are ultimately responsible for executing that strategy?

An effective business strategy summary typically includes the following components:

- A summary of your organization's strengths and weaknesses, along with the opportunities and threats you see
- Your vision, mission, and values
- The top business goals of the organization that, if achieved, will drive your success
- The individual strategies that will help you achieve those goals
- The measurement components for each strategy

And don't forget to leave space for individual leaders to customize the organizational information for their teams.

MISTAKE

You create a
theme along with
your strategy that's
more about talking
to yourself than to
your core audiences

I heard an interesting comparison recently. When you see people on the street talking to themselves, they are often classified as "insane." Yet what do we call it when we talk to ourselves inside organizations? "Marketing or communications."

Unfortunately, that type of talking to oneself—where leaders speak *TO* their own understanding and perspectives instead of engaging *WITH* employees—happens too frequently. And the consequences can be staggering. The first misstep many leaders make is packaging their business strategy into a neat theme, slogan or logo that has no real connection with the strategy itself. As long as it looks pretty or sounds catchy, employees will "get it." Right? **Wrong.**

Every interaction with employees is a precious chance to make sure they're working hard on behalf of the business. Distracting them with a theme or logo that doesn't mean anything is simply a lost opportunity to connect, foster dialogue, answer questions and any number of best practices that inspire and motivate employees.

So you have your strategy in place. And now you want to introduce it to employees, along with a key theme. Ask these questions:

- Does the theme resonate with your employees? Can they see themselves in it, or is it something only senior-most leaders will understand or identify with?
- Does it help drive the behaviors you want to see in every last employee?
- Is it easily adaptable or customizable for business units or geographies to continue to drive relevance further down in your organization?
- Does it connect to your larger organizational branding?
- Have you tested your theme with employees and adapted it based on their feedback?

Talking *TO* employees is a lot easier than talking *WITH* them. Make sure everything associated with your strategy—from the words that describe it, to the theme or logo that represents it—resonates with those very people on whom you're relying for success. That's turning "talking to ourselves" into true "communications."

MISTAKE

You don't hold your leaders accountable to communicate your strategy

The most effective leaders distinguish themselves through effective communication. While it's likely very few leaders would dispute that concept, even fewer seem to take it to heart and use communication to their advantage. Why? One word. Accountability.

Leaders in any organization and at all levels are held to high standards and judged by their performance in important areas impacting the business: sales, operations, marketing, efficiency, development of their people, and so on. But they're not held accountable for communicating with employees, which is arguably the foundation for success for every one of those areas listed in the previous sentence!

Leaders set the tone for how information flows inside an organization and how employees work and interact together, yet many aren't judged on their performance in this critical discipline.

Accountability must be built in at multiple levels so leaders know what is expected of them, understand what "success" looks like, and can perform effectively to meet the stated expectations. When set up best, accountability for communication is part of the overall performance management system and is specifically tied to compensation.

In a global organization, accountability might rest with a local leader responsible for communicating with employees in a specific facility; with a regional or country leader who must interpret company strategy for a given geography; and with a global leader whose role includes aligning groups from diverse backgrounds around the company's mission, vision and values.

No matter what the task, expectations are clearly outlined so leadership can step up to the plate and are motivated to do so because it's in their best interest.

MISTAKE

You don't arm leaders with the training and tools they need to communicate the strategy and make it relevant for their teams

It's one thing to hold leaders accountable for communications about the business strategy, but it's another to fail to support them with the right training and tools to help facilitate it.

Training ensures a leader builds the competence needed to customize and communicate critical information, and there's no more critical piece of information than your business strategy. This training could include programs to help leaders understand and leverage strategic communication, workshops in which they share best practices on typical communication defining moments such as how to use a communication toolkit on the organizational strategy, or individualized coaching from counselors to provide feedback and help them hone their communication skills. Since leadership communication is a learned skill, this is a critical element. When leaders know better, they do better.

Tools provide leaders with what they need to get their message across to various audiences. These often are compiled in a standard kit that leaders can pull from and customize for communicating in different settings and circumstances, whether its bullet points for a casual lunch with employees or a presentation on the company's key goals for a sales event or all-staff meeting. There might also be a tool that highlights the key leadership behaviors that will have the most impact in delivering an important message, such as face-to-face or small-group communications vs. other vehicles.

Finally, leaders need to be assessed. How are they doing at meeting the expectations you've set for them?

I call it the *Core Four:* accountability, tools, training, and measurement. Miss one, and you've reduced your chances of moving leaders to action.

MISTAKE

You don't translate the strategy into local language for teams across the globe

Working with global clients who need to communicate with employees around the world, I've been hearing a lot lately about the challenges of translation. This issue is not likely to go away any time soon as more companies see opportunities and set goals to grow their international business.

We see clients struggle with the best way to send and receive timely information to engage employees in multiple languages and cultures. We hear from employees who feel frustrated because they want to receive information in their native language, with the same immediacy as they receive it in English.

My own experience reinforces how we need to be aware of our individual points of view when working with people from other cultures and languages. Recently, when conducting employee focus groups in Germany, I knew I had to slow down my typical rapid speech and be cognizant of the slang that's so prevalent in the English language. But I also discovered the need to explain the terms "focus group" and "guidelines," neither of which exists in German, to help attendees understand the goals of the session and how a focus group works.

It reminded me that it is critical—regardless of where you are and with whom you deal—to establish a shared understanding with stakeholders. This is important even with fellow English-speakers, who often come to the table from different backgrounds and geographies. You think about a topic in a certain way based on your personal experience, while I think about it based on my experience. We could be talking about the same thing and not understand each other at all because we are coming at the concepts in a very different way. The potential for misunderstanding increases when language differences enter the mix.

Whatever the specific issues and situations you face with people of different cultures, it's important to find common ground and recognize that senders and receivers share the same goals. They all seek to understand their company's objectives and needs, and they all want to be effective at their jobs.

To be sure your internal communications don't get lost in translation, consider these solutions:

Make sure mission-critical information is translated.
Across the globe, people need to have a common understanding of the vision and business goals, along with their role in achieving them. This should be communicated in their native language. Many organizations identify the key 10-12 languages most common in their organization and translate mission-critical information accordingly.

If you want an employee to do something, translate the communication.
Employees can't contribute if they don't understand the message and how they can help—not to mention what's in it for them.

Create a quality-control process that ensures accurate translation.
Translate material locally to address cultural nuances, but coordinate all translations centrally to ensure the broader company message and meaning are getting through.

Support communication with dialogue.
Incorporate face-to-face conversations and feedback techniques into your communication process to build a foundation of understanding and to help you know whether you are in sync with your audience. When addressing a complex topic, start at the broadest, highest strategic level and ensure understanding there first, then go deeper.

Give employees the choice of language.

Don't assume you know the language your employees want to use. Give them the option to get materials in the language of their choice to best ensure the messages resonate. Doing so also allows you to merchandise your translation efforts and get "credit" from employees for communicating in ways that are most relevant to them. It's an investment to translate materials into multiple languages, so make the most of the opportunity to let employees know you care about their needs.

Define critical terminology.

When you are using specific words that you want understood and repeated consistently, ask questions to ensure you and your employee audience are defining terms in the same way. For example, you might start by agreeing that your organization wants to grow and be profitable, then you could discuss what that means to the audience. In this case, questions like, "What does 'grow' mean?" or "What does 'profitable' look like in the context of this organization (what are the targets, milestones, how are we growing)?" can help individuals relate to the larger goals.

Focus on what your audience is saying.

Check for understanding with occasional clarifying questions such as, "How would you explain what I've just told you?" or "Could you share your understanding of this approach?" When you ask people to paraphrase back to you what they've heard, you know where they are coming from and whether they have received the message or not. And just as important, the questions people ask tell you what they are thinking and how much they are connecting with your message.

MISTAKE

You have a strategy, but there isn't a way for the areas of your business to internalize and personalize it to their work

A great strategy means nothing if it can't be implemented. Hundreds of organizations fail to succeed because they do a poor job at interpreting the strategy for employees and fail to give them the tools and resources they need to execute.

The organizational strategy needs to be customized at all levels of your organization—so leaders in APMEA, for example, can develop and articulate how the strategy is brought to life in their part of the world. So countries in Asia Pacific can customize their strategies based on the APMEA and global strategy. And so on.

Each level—through the front-line employee—needs to be able to articulate how they bring the strategy to life. In other words, how they fit in and contribute. That's all about making the strategy relevant—and answering that all-important "what's in it for me question," too.

When it comes to activating strategy, if everyone can articulate how they fit in, you're going to accelerate your ability to deliver on that strategy. No small task, but well worth the effort.

"Individual commitment to a group effort—that is what makes a team work, a company work, a society work, a civilization work."

– Vince Lombardi, Football Coach

You don't tie all your communications to an element of the strategy

If your strategy is your North Star, then all your communications should explicitly link to an element of the strategy so employees understand how what they do connects. This also reinforces the importance of the strategy.

Reviewing an agenda for the next senior leadership meeting? How does it explicitly reinforce the strategy and goals? Too many agendas are updates on what's been accomplished by departments or regions instead of updates as they relate to critical areas of the strategy.

Want to recognize someone for their results? As you share appreciative feedback, make sure to connect the results back to one of your core values and behaviors.

Sharing a business update at an all-employee meeting? Use the strategy as an organizing factor for your remarks, and mention explicitly each of the core components of the strategy.

"One man can be a crucial ingredient on a team, but one man cannot make a team."

– Kareem Abdul-Jabbar, retired NBA star

At its core, great leadership is all about giving direction, offering context, and ensuring that every person in the company—from the representative on the front lines of customer service to members of the senior leadership team—understands in ways that are relevant to him or her what the company strategy is, what it will take to accomplish its goals, and what the rewards are when you get there.

All that can only happen through communication.

Though communication does not always get the attention it deserves in C-suite planning, great leaders know it's at the heart of their success—*it's the leavening that makes the strategic bread rise, the wheels that make the strategic car drive, the brush with which you paint your masterpiece.* You get the idea…

It's remarkable what you can accomplish when people know where you're going and how to get there.

TRY IT TODAY

- Be literal when defining your strategy. Define all key terms, even if the meaning seems obvious to you.

- Answer the "what's in it for me" question that all employees ask. This will help them understand how they fit into the bigger picture—the business strategy— and help drive engagement.

- Spend available time with employees. Allocate time to walk the halls and eat lunch in the cafeteria. Getting employees' thoughts on the job will help you best understand how your strategy is being communicated.

- Share feedback and connect positive results back to one of your core values and behaviors.

Evaluation

Starting thought

How to know you're communicating well

I was talking with a client recently about how you know you're getting your message across in a one-on-one situation, especially when you have a good amount of material to present.

One of the best ways to gauge understanding is by the questions your employees ask. But how do you know before then? The answer is simple: look for any kind of movement from the person you're speaking with. Chances are a look away, a glance down, or nodding is a clue you'll want to be aware of.

That's your signal to check for understanding by asking a question: "We've covered a lot of information so far; how do you feel about what we discussed?" Or, "How does this fit with how you see the current situation?" Any question that opens dialogue (hint: ensure you ask open-ended questions vs. a yes/no question) will help you know where your audience stands.

When you know where your audience is coming from, you're best able to be persuasive, because you can adapt your messages based on the feedback you're getting. That's the core of any great conversation that leads to shared meaning and, as always, to the results you want.

How do you react to what I just shared?

Feedback Can Help You (Get Back and) Stay On Track

When was the last time you asked your employees for feedback?

Most leaders aren't afraid to give feedback, either solicited or unsolicited. Getting feedback about yourself can be a different story.

Hearing what your employees think about the decisions you make and the actions you take can help guide what you say and do in the future and is a significant credibility booster when done well.

In a one-on-one setting, you might ask employees to complete the following fill-in-the-blank statement, "You can be better if…" The leader's job is to listen, absorb, and then ask, "How else could I be better?" Continue listening and asking questions until your employee runs out of suggestions. Thank them for their candid input. Resist the desire to get defensive in any way. Remember, you can always loop back with the employee at a later date on issues that need dialogue.

Leaders may not always like what they hear, but open, honest feedback is sometimes the best way to take the pulse of your organization and its people—not to mention to know how you can even better support your employees in the future.

TIP:

Q. What's one of the best ways to know whether your presentation or communication was well received and understood?

A. By the questions people ask. If they're basic questions that get at the core of what you communicated, you somehow missed the mark.

If they're forward-looking or more detail-oriented questions, you can rest assured your team is with you. They got the message and are even thinking ahead as to what's next.

An Ending Question That's Really a Beginning
Want to check for understanding in a larger group setting?

Here's a helpful phrase any leader can use to set yourself up for success: "I know I've covered a great deal in the last few minutes. What questions do you have of me? Anything I can elaborate on? What can I clarify for you?" Then, wait.

Instead of asking, "Any questions?" you're much more specific, which shows you're open and welcoming to questions and dialogue. Use this strategy at natural breaks in your presentation or about every five to ten minutes.

Be Open to Open-Ended Questions
If you've ever tried to ask teenagers about their day only to get a response of "fine," you know the importance of asking the right kind of open-ended questions to encourage dialogue.

Try these questions to spark dialogue:

- What were your key takeaways from the meeting we had today?
- What else can I do to help you understand this topic?
- What questions do you have? Who'd like to go first?
- How did this experience leave you feeling?
- From what I shared with you today, what do you think this means for you?
- What thoughts do you have that would help me be better next time?

CHAPTER 12

There's no Loophole Here...Always Close the Loop

When employees share their thoughts and feedback, the leader's work is just beginning. This is the time when leaders need to take action on the feedback and close the loop with employees about those actions so they have proof that their input was heard and valued.

Employees will be more willing to share their feedback in the future if they know their input is heard and acted on, or if not acted on, that they understand why.

If you're changing how you communicated based on feedback from employees, let them know what you're doing and why. They'll know you heard them and value their perspective.

For larger communication efforts, consider whether a survey would be appropriate to allow employees to share their feedback confidentially. And, on completion of the survey, always report the key headlines and actions being taken as a result of the survey.

Look in the Mirror

Whenever you deliver messages, spend a few minutes to look in your own mirror to reflect on your communication and assess if you had the impact you wanted.

Ask yourself...

- Did I take the time to plan my communications?

- How did I feel delivering the messages? Did I feel prepared or was I "winging it?"

- Did I listen more than I talked?

- Was there a two-way conversation, or did it feel like I talked the whole time?

- Did I check for understanding?

- Did I get the reaction from employees that I'd hoped?

- What questions did people ask?

- Am I seeing a change in people's actions?

TRY IT TODAY

- The best way to know if employees understand what you're saying is through the questions they ask. Today, listen to the kinds of questions people ask and determine if your communications are missing or hitting the mark.

- Getting feedback is a powerful tool to improve your communication. Ask for it at your next meeting with open-ended questions.

- Reflect on your own communications to see what worked and what you could do even better next time.

Closing Thought

Sink or swim?

The uncommon realities of communication

While many of the strategies in this book may seem like common sense—*and they are*—they're not common practice. If you treat employees with respect, as adults, and follow the Golden Rule, you'll be off to a good start. But effective communication takes so much more.

Engaging employees, creating a shared vision, inspiring your team, and moving them to action are more difficult, but provide a significant opportunity for you—the leader—and for your staff.

I love the Dr. Seuss book, *Oh, the Places You'll Go,* which celebrates life's journey as only the incomparable Dr. Seuss can: "You have brains in your head. You have feet in your shoes. You can steer yourself any direction you choose."

And if you're ever wondering about how you'll do on the path less-traveled: "Will you succeed? Yes, you will indeed. (98 3/4% guaranteed.)"

Developing sound communication skills will take you places you never thought you would go, and those who successfully climb the ladder realize the critical need to be adept at communications. It's often hard to convince leaders how important communication is until they begin the journey and see and feel the results themselves.

My father passed away from pancreatic cancer a number of years back. It's a club to which many of us belong—having loved ones who are affected by cancer—a club in which no one wants membership.

My dad had a wonderful sense of humor. He was a quiet man and rarely said much, but when he did talk, you took notice. Nine times out of ten, he shared a pun. Most were groaners; a standout few made me laugh out loud. (I'm fortunate to have inherited his wicked pun gene.)

A few days before he died, we moved him to a wonderful hospice in Milwaukee, Wisconsin, called St. Mary's Hospice, and he was cared for by nurses who I swore were angels.

He was heavily sedated and not very responsive in his last few days, but all of us at his bedside still spoke to him as if he could hear us. And deep inside, I believed he could.

I'll never forget the day the rabbi was coming to visit. My mom leaned over and whispered to my dad, "Gordie," she said, "the rabbi will be here today, do you want me to take down the cross?"

Before I could burst out laughing, my dad opened his eyes for the first time in days. For that single moment, time stopped for me. A silence grew over the room, all of us wondering what would happen next. And, without missing a beat, my dad said, "Gloria, don't touch that cross. I can use all the help I can get right now!"

It was an important lesson for me. You never know where life will take you and where help might come from when you're open to the journey.

A former CEO I used to work for always said, "Jump in. The water's fine."

I never could swim very well. But I always was willing to jump. And the rest has taken care of itself.

Dad would be proud.

1. Lumesse, "Global Workplace Study" (June 2011)

2. Towers Watson, "Capitalizing on Effective Communication: Communication ROI Study Report" (2009/2010)

3. IDC Research, "$37 Billion: Counting the Cost of Employee Misunderstanding" (2008)

4. IDC Research, ibid

5. SIS International Research for Siemens Communications, "Communications Pain Study: Uncovering the hidden cost of communications barriers and latency" (2009)

6. Forbes Insights, "Talent Edge 2020: Building the recovery together" (2011)

7. Towers Watson "WorkUSA Survey" (2008/2009)

8. Towers Watson, ibid

9. Gallup, Inc., Gallup Management Journal (October 2006)

10. Towers Watson, "Global Workforce Study" (2007/2008)

11. Towers Watson, "O.C. Tanner 2008 Global Recognition Study" (2008)

12. Towers Watson, "Capitalizing on Effective Communication: Communication ROI Study Report" (2009/2010)

13. International Association of Business Communicators and Best Consulting, "Employee Engagement Survey" (2011)

14. International Association of Business Communicators (IABC), "Best Practices in Employee Communication: A Study of Global Challenges and Approaches" (2005)

15. IABC, ibid

16. Institute of Internal Communication (IoIC), United Kingdom, online survey of internal communicators (2011)

17. IoIC, ibid

18. IoIC, ibid

19. James Harter and Rodd Wagner, "12: The Elements of Great Managing" (2006)

20. Maritz Research, "Employee Engagement Poll, Annual Attitude Survey" (2011)

21. Towers Watson, "O.C. Tanner 2008 Global Recognition Study" (2008)

22. Edelman, "Trust Barometer, Global Opinion Leaders Study" (2010)

23. Edelman, "Trust Barometer, Global Opinion Leaders Study" (2011)

24. Internal IBM Branding Study (2010)

25. Towers Perrin, "Turbocharging Employee Engagement" (2005)

26. Allen Schweyer, "The Economics of Engagement" (2008)

27. Watson Wyatt, "Increasing Employee Engagement: Strategies for Enhancing Business and Individual Performance – 2007/2008 WorkAsia™ Survey Report" (2008)

28. Dr. David Sirota, "The Enthusiastic Employee: How Companies Profit by Giving Workers What They Want" (2004)

29. Institute for Corporate Productivity (i4cp), "Employee Turnover and Engagement Pulse Survey" (September 2009)

30. Jim Collins, Good to Great (Random House, 2001)

31. The Grossman Group, national telephone survey of 420 adults in the U.S. who are employed and have supervisors (August 2009)

32. John F. Helliwell, "Speech to the Vancouver Board of Trade, Launch of Knowledge for the Boardroom" (March 2006)

33. Strategic HR Review, "The Three Dimensions of Engagement," Volume 4 Issue 2 (2005)

34. Stephen M.R. Covey with Rebecca R. Merrill, The SPEED of Trust: The One Thing That Changes Everything (Free Press, 2008)

35. Weber-Shandwick, Survey (October 2008)

36. International Association of Business Communicators (IABC), "Best Practices in Employee Communication: A Study of Global Challenges and Approaches" (2005)

37. Harvard Business Review, "What Only the CEO Can Do" (May 2009)

Would you like David to present a powerful program to your organization?

David Grossman is a much sought-after speaker and consultant, acclaimed for his highly engaging, interactive, and powerful programs. He's known for his thoughtful, personal, and pragmatic approach that leverages communication as one of the ultimate business tools.

From Fortune 100 companies to professional associations and universities, David's proven leadership communication programs benefit leaders at all levels and help them connect the dots between communication and business results.

To request a speaker's kit or for more information, please visit: www.yourthoughtpartner.com/speaking-and-events

?

Give Us Feedback on *You Can't Not Communicate*

We're interested in what you think. What was most helpful? Least helpful?

What's working for you that we should share with others?

What new challenges do you face today?

E-mail us your thoughts at **results@yourthoughtpartner.com**.

David Grossman

ABC, APR, Fellow PRSA, is both a teacher and student of effective communication. He is one of America's foremost authorities on communication inside organizations.

Known for his thoughtful, personal, and pragmatic approach, David coaches leaders at all levels to utilize communication as a strategic business tool. The "anti-social media guy," David addresses both the importance of effective internal and leadership communication and the critical need for face-to-face communication amid the surge of electronic media. By acting as an advocate for employees and a **thought**partner to senior management, David and his team help organizations unleash the power of communication to engage employees and drive performance.

Leveraging his background in organizational development and psychology, David facilitates training programs developed exclusively for senior leadership teams at Fortune 500 companies and other leading organizations. David also answers leadership and employee communication questions everyday through his "Ask David" iPhone application.

His second book, *"You Can't **NOT** Communicate **2: More** Proven Communication Solutions That Power the Fortune 100"* has received accolades and praise from leaders, communication professionals, and educators for "reminding leaders (everywhere and at all levels) of the importance of getting communication right" and for providing "proven and practical insights, methods, and tools" to enhance results and ensure overall engagement.

David currently teaches the only graduate-level course in internal communications in the U.S. at Columbia University. He has been published in numerous industry journals and is the author of *"Internal Branding: How to*

Create and Sustain a Successful Internal Brand," "The Practitioner's Guide to Essential Techniques for Employee Engagement," and the CD-ROM *"message**maps***: *A Guide to Creating Clear, Credible and Impactful Messages."*

David was recently named to *USA Today's* corporate management and leadership CEO panel. In 2009, he was a finalist for the NGLCC Wells Fargo Business Owner of the Year Award, honoring his entrepreneurial spirit for business performance, innovation, growth, and personal service to the community. He is a member of the National Speakers Association and is a designated IABC recommended speaker.

Prior to founding The Grossman Group in 2000, David was director of communications for McDonald's. David graduated summa cum laude, Phi Beta Kappa from the University of Wisconsin-Madison with an honors degree in journalism and holds a master's in Corporate Public Relations from Northwestern University. He began his career as a journalist, working in radio news and television.

THE
GROSSMAN
GROUP

About The Grossman Group

Twice named *PR Week's* "Boutique Agency of the Year" and *The Holmes Report's* "Employee Communication Agency of the Year," The Grossman Group (www.yourthoughtpartner.com) is an award-winning Chicago-based communications consultancy focusing on organizational consulting, strategic leadership development, and internal communications.

The Grossman Group's client roster includes Fortune 500 clients such as Accor, Apollo Group, Cisco, Geisinger, Heinz, HTC, Intel, LifeScan, Lilly, Lockheed Martin, MassMutual, McDonald's, Microsoft, Pioneer Hi-Bred, Rockwell Automation, UNUM and Virgin Atlantic.

Using its unique Grossman Methodology—encompassing its award-winning proprietary tools, training and **thought**partner approach—the consultancy delivers proven, breakthrough strategies that solve clients' business challenges, especially around:

- Minimizing the downside of change when business could be interrupted, slowed, or stopped

- Turning employee confusion, skepticism, and apathy into productivity and engagement

- Maximizing the upside of change to accelerate business results

The Grossman Group is a certified diversity supplier through the National Gay and Lesbian Chamber of Commerce (NGLCC). In 2010, The Grossman Group was named by DiversityBusiness.com as one of the top 500 diversity-owned businesses in the U.S. The Grossman Group's work has won all the "Oscars" of communications—the prestigious Silver Anvil Award from the Public Relations Society of America (PRSA), the Gold Quill Award from the International Association of Business Communicators (IABC), the Golden World Award from the International Public Relations Association (IPRA), and SABRE Awards from The Holmes Report.

Be Connected

Visit Our Website

Go to www.yourthoughtpartner.com to learn more about The Grossman Group and its proven approach to strategic leadership and internal communication. Also download free eBooks such as *"Mastering the Art of Messaging"* and *"Going Slow to Go Fast: Making Internal Communications Work for You."*

Subscribe to ethoughtstarters

For quick, simple tips to help build better leader**communicators** subscribe to our **e**thought**starters** newsletter by visiting www.yourthoughtpartner.com/ethought-starters.

Participate in the Discussion

To see what others are saying on the latest topics and issues around communication and to post your own thoughts, check out David's blog at www.yourthoughtpartner.com/blog. You can also engage on LinkedIn and through David's "Ask David" app for iPhone and Droid.

Get Quantity Discounts

Books are available at quantity discounts on orders of 50 copies or more. Please call us at 312.829.3252, visit us online at www.yourthoughtpartner.com/book or email office@yourthoughtpartner.com.

Invite David to Speak

To help your leaders at all levels be better communicators, invite David to speak to groups large and small by going to www.yourthoughtpartner.com/speaking-and-events.

Stay Connected

Thousands of readers continue to receive communication tools and best practices from David. You can do so too, by subscribing to the leader**communicator** blog or by following David on Twitter at @ThoughtPartner.

Building off the highly-acclaimed *You Can't **Not** Communicate*, David's second book, *You Can't **Not** Communicate **2**: **More** Proven Communication Solutions that Power the Fortune 100*, tackles some of today's most critical, but less commonplace business challenges facing leaders, including understanding employee needs to drive engagement, motivating Millennials, and engaging hard-to-reach employees.

With a variety of new leader insights, proven communication solutions, and real-time approaches with 'try it today' lessons, *You Can't **Not** Communicate **2*** will help propel any leader to the next level.

Featuring a foreword by Olivier Poirot, SVP and CFO, Sodexo Noram *(former CEO, Accor North America)*

www.yourthoughtpartner.com/book

YOU CAN'T **NOT** COMMUN CATE 2

More ^ Proven Communication Solutions that Power the Fortune 100

HOW TOP LEADERS **DIFFERENTIATE THEMSELVES**

by **DAVID GROSSMAN**, ABC, APR, Fellow PRSA

foreword by OLIVIER POIROT, CEO, Accor North America

> ❝ David Grossman's combination of instinctual perception and practical advice is rare. Whether you're new to your organization or a veteran, whether you're driving change or honing what you have, Grossman's insight will accelerate your efforts. ❞
>
> — *John Greisch, CEO,*
> *Hill-Rom Holdings, Inc.*

> ❝ Practical, wise, smartly designed— an example of what it recommends to its readers. ❞
>
> — *Jon Iwata, Senior Vice President,*
> *Marketing and Communications,*
> *IBM Corporation*